# SEA OVER BOW

A Prince Edward Islander

in the Royal Canadian Naval Volunteer Reserve

in World War II.

LAWSON DRAKE

*Lawson Drake*

*Vernon Drake*

*For Earl —*
*I hope you enjoy my yarn.*
*Lawson*

Canadian Cataloguing in Publication Data

Drake, Lawson, 1930-

Sea over bow

Includes bibliographical references.
ISBN 0-9687871-0-X

1. Drake, Lawson, 1930-  2. Royal Canadian Naval Volunteer Reserve –
Biography. 3. World War, 1939-1945 – Naval operations,Canadian. 4.
World War, 1939-1945 – Personal narratives, Canadian. 5. Sailors –
Prince Edward Island – Biography. I. Title.

D811.D72 2000   940.54'5971"092    C00-950225-4

# CONTENTS

# SUPREME HEADQUARTERS
## ALLIED EXPEDITIONARY FORCE

**Soldiers, Sailors and Airmen of the Allied Expeditionary Force!**

You are about to embark upon the Great Crusade, toward which we have striven these many months. The eyes of the world are upon you. The hopes and prayers of liberty-loving people everywhere march with you. In company with our brave Allies and brothers-in-arms on other Fronts, you will bring about the destruction of the German war machine, the elimination of Nazi tyranny over the oppressed peoples of Europe, and security for ourselves in a free world.

Your task will not be an easy one. Your enemy is well trained, well equipped and battle-hardened. He will fight savagely.

But this is the year 1944 ! Much has happened since the Nazi triumphs of 1940-41. The United Nations have inflicted upon the Germans great defeats, in open battle, man-to-man. Our air offensive has seriously reduced their strength in the air and their capacity to wage war on the ground. Our Home Fronts have given us an overwhelming superiority in weapons and munitions of war, and placed at our disposal great reserves of trained fighting men. The tide has turned ! The free men of the world are marching together to Victory !

I have full confidence in your courage, devotion to duty and skill in battle. We will accept nothing less than full Victory !

Good Luck ! And let us all beseech the blessing of Almighty God upon this great and noble undertaking.

*Dwight Eisenhower*

*Message from the Supreme Allied Commander, General Eisenhower, to all personnel participating in the invasion of Normandy June 6, 1944.*

# PREFACE.

The survivors of the young men who went to war in Canada's Army, Navy and Air Force in World War II are now old men. Each year, on November 11, we honour them and join with them in honouring the memories of their comrades who were killed on active service. But most of us do so without having any clear sense of what it meant to be "on active service". While there are many excellent books telling of the chaos of battle, of heroism in the face of the enemy, of the pathos of death and of the bittersweet reality of survival, for every story told in those books, countless others are untold.

It may be presumptuous of me to set out to tell one more story; perhaps I am just carrying to extremes a small boy's one time hero worship of his big brother in the Navy. But I genuinely believe that every war veteran's experience is worth telling and retelling so that his or her contribution to freedom never be lost to the memory of men. So I set out to tell my brother's story. He joined the navy as a lad of eighteen, and served more than five years. In one respect his naval service differed from that of the great majority of sea-going Canadians in World War II: all his sea time was in large ships. He did not sail in any of those gallant small vessels - minesweepers, corvettes and frigates - in which so many young men went to sea trying to protect convoys of merchant ships against the depredations of German submarines.

I began by recording his recollections of more than a half century ago. What was surprising was not that his recall was less than total, nor that at times the temporal sequence of events was confused; it was that his memory was still so vivid. By reading various accounts of the actions and campaigns in which his ships participated and by consulting ship's log books I was able to corroborate his stories and establish the correct chronology of events. By talking to some of his shipmates and through reading the letters and diaries of others I gleaned additional information which not only gave me a clearer idea of his life at sea but helped Vernon to recall incidents which he had not thought about for many years. Finally, by visiting the World War II cruiser HMS *Belfast*, preserved for the nation by the Imperial War Museum in London, I gained some impression of what it must have been like to be a crewman in a fighting ship.

Readers seeking heroics will be disappointed. What follows is a story of what I call ordinary valour, as distinct from the more talked about, the more noticed kind - extraordinary valour - the kind that is recognized by commendations and medals. Ordinary valour was a prerequisite for life at sea in wartime because that life comprised days stretching into weeks, prolonged to months and even years, of living close to danger: danger that lurked below the surface of the calmest sea; that hid behind the whitest of clouds; that waited just over the nearest horizon. No man knew when danger would strike. Sailors lived in cramped, closed-up spaces, storm-buffeted, often wet, sometimes cold, sometimes hot, short of sleep and indifferently fed, their only tangible enemy the sea itself. Then, in a single explosive instant, life could assume dimensions of incredible tension and terror as alarm bells and the call to "Action Stations!" triggered violent action and the imminence of death.

As a seaman in the Royal Canadian Naval Volunteer Reserve, my brother, Vernon Drake, lived that life, with brief respites, for more than four years during World War II. His memories of those years are the thread with which I have tried to knit together a number of tales into the story which follows.

Some persons, having read the manuscript, have observed that it seems to contain two stories: Vernon's, and another which I fashioned out of my reading. I counter these comments by saying that, if at times Vernon tends to disappear from the narrative it is only because, as an individual naval rating, his life was bound over to circumstances often unknown to him, and to forces over which he had no control. From my reading I have tried to explain some of those circumstances and identify some of those forces, so as to place him, and you the reader, in the larger world beyond his ship. For Vernon's world was his ship; as a member of her crew he was a part of everything she did. Her life was his life; his fate was tied to her fate. When his ship was in peril, he was in peril. When his ship went to Action Stations, he was at Action Stations, at his gun, in a high state of readiness for whatever his ship might encounter.

I dedicate this story to him and to the other boys of Meadow Bank who, putting boyhood aside, answered as men the call to armed service, 1939 to 1945.

Lawson Drake,
Meadow Bank, P.E.I.
April, 2000.

# MEADOW BANK'S ROLL OF HONOUR, 1939 - 1945.

**Terris Miller**, Flight Sergeant (W.A.G.)     RCAF
       Killed in action over Belgium,
       August 28, 1942, age 23

| | |
|---|---|
| Vernon Drake | RCNVR |
| Eric MacFadyen | RCNVR |
| Norman MacFadyen | VETERAN'S GUARD |
| Harvey MacLean | RCNVR |
| Reigh MacLean | RCNVR |
| Henry (Harry) Miller | RCEME |
| John Miller | RCA |
| Waldie Miller | RCNVR |
| Walter (Bertie) Miller | RCA |
| Orville Murray | RCNVR |

Enlisted from another community, lived in Meadow Bank post-war.

| | |
|---|---|
| Jean (Morley) MacLean | WRCNS |
| Norma (Walker) MacLean | WAAF |
| Dorothy (Agnew) Yeo | RAMC |
| James Yeo | RCA |

# ACKNOWLEDGEMENTS.

Many people helped me with this book. To them all I offer sincere thanks: to Vernon Drake, Frank Carragher, Jim Grady, Patrick Horgan, Joe LeClair and Jack Thomson, who by generously sharing their experiences with me, gave me the basic material for the book; to Kay Horgan for lending me her scrapbook, and for putting me in the way of Robert Cross' diary; to Frances and Rosemary Curley for giving me a copy of Janet Christian's essay, *Ships I Have Sailed and Bastards I Have Known: A Glimpse of World War Two Through the Eyes of An Island Navy Veteran.*, the reminiscences of Richard Curley; to Robert Crawford, Director-General, and Peter Simkins, Chief Historian, Imperial War Museum, for service records of HMS *Glasgow* and other HM ships and for copies of Able Seaman R.E. Hughes' diary and Lieut. Comm. R.C. McNab's letter; to Commander C. J. Balfour, D.L., for extracts from his Midshipman's log; to Jon Wenzell, Director of HMS *Belfast*, for conducting me through the ship and answering innumerable questions.

Hon. Roy MacLaren, P.C.,Canadian High Commissioner to the United KIngdom, deserves a special thanks for his encouragement, for helping me to contact the right people at the Imperial War Museum, and for reading the manuscript and offering valued editorial comments. Equally deserving of thanks for reading the manuscript and for their perceptive editing are Ian Brown, C.W.J. Eliot, Carolyn Drake, John Drake, Allison Jay and Allan Jay. All of them suggested improvements to the text and none are in any way responsible for remaining errors; such are attributable to me alone.

I thank the Imperial War Muscum for permission to use the pictures relating to HMS *Glasgow* and the National Archives of Canada for permission to use the pictures relating to HMCS *Uganda*.

I am grateful to the Cultural Development Program, Department of Community Services and Attorney General, for a grant in aid of production.

Lastly, and of all the most deserving of my thanks, is my wife Eileen, who endured my long hours of preoccupation, my days and weeks "on the computer", and whose insistence was the final impetus for bringing this book to completion.

# *FOREWORD*

*Sea Over Bow* is a book that needed to be written and needs to be read. The author, Lawson Drake, asserts that he set out simply to recount the story of his older brother, Vernon's, experience in the Royal Canadian Naval Volunteer Reserve. With an uncanny knack of capturing the essence of events as they unfolded and as his brother experienced them, the author has covered an enormous naval canvas which encompasses almost every ocean and continent on the globe. Overlaid on this vast geography are most of the major naval wartime operations. The book is a delight to read and contains an exceptional level of authentic information which will surprise even the most seasoned readers.

*Sea Over Bow* gives a superb overview of one Islander's five years of almost continuous sea-time in cruiser-sized warships. Much has been written about the small Canadian ships of World War II. The corvettes on the North Atlantic convoy run, foul weather, U-Boats, Wolf Packs and impossible living conditions at sea were all part of these stories. Now the author, through his brother's eyes, has recounted a story about larger warships - the cruisers. In these supposedly "grand" ships the above noted evils of the small ships of the North Atlantic were all present, plus the suffocating heat of the tropics, very long periods at sea, totally inadequate and unsuitable food and, in the end, woefully inept political decisions by Canada.

Through his brother's experiences the author takes his readers from Meadow Bank, P.E.I. to the far reaches of the South Pacific and back. It is one hell of a trip! It is possible that, having made that trip, Vernon Drake is the first Drake since Sir Francis to have circumnavigated the globe.

Vice-Admiral James C. Wood
CMM, CD, RCN (Retired)
September 14, 2000

**Arthur Vernon Drake**

Born Meadow Bank, Prince Edward Island, September 22, 1921.
Enlisted Royal Canadian Naval Volunteer Reserve, July 2, 1940, Service
Number V1337.
HMCS *Prince David* December 28, 1940 - April 30, 1943.
HMCS *Glasgow* December 31, 1943 - July 9, 1944.
HMCS *Uganda* August 31, 1944 - August 9, 1945.
Honorable Discharge as Leading Seaman, October 22, 1945.

# 1. IN THE BEGINNING: FARM BOY TO ORDINARY SEAMAN.

The war clouds gathering over Europe in the summer of 1939 had not risen far above Prince Edward Island's horizon - or if they had, very few Islanders had noticed them. In a still predominantly rural province the main pre-occupation was with the crops - their planting, growth and harvest. In June there was considerable stir attending the visit of Their Majesties, King George the Sixth and Queen Elizabeth, but the excitement was manifested more by the school children who lined Charlottetown's streets to catch a glimpse of passing royalty and by the "bigwigs" who milled about a sodden garden party at Government House, than by the majority of the country people. Few of the thousands who cheered the royal couple in Charlottetown realized that this visit was a rallying cry to the Empire about to be sorely tested, and that the sovereign's Canadian Naval escort, the destroyers HMCS *Skeena* and *Saguenay*, would, within the year, be joining battle with a skilled and relentless undersea enemy, the German U-Boat navy.

In that summer of 1939 Vernon Drake had not yet reached his eighteenth birthday. The second of three sons born to Lemuel Drake and Carrie MacLaren, he had grown up on his parents' farm in Meadow Bank, a quiet rural community on the banks of the Eliot and Clyde rivers a few miles from Charlottetown. He had attended school until he was fifteen years old and then, because farm incomes were low, he looked for work away from home. A young man such as he, if he could get a job, might earn as much as eighteen to twenty dollars a month. Vernon found such work in the nearby village of Cornwall, work that kept him going twelve to sixteen hours a day, six days a week, driving a truck, doing farm work and odd jobs for an employer whose day started at sunrise and stretched well beyond the fall of darkness. Vernon was supposed to get his pay every Saturday night, but he often had to wait into the next week before getting his five dollar weekly wages. It was not a life with a future, especially for someone whose education had ceased at grade eight. But it was still the tail end of the Depression and it could be argued that a fellow was lucky to have any kind of employment.

Then came the war. On September 3, 1939, his diplomacy a sorry failure as the German blitzkrieg rolled over the Polish frontier, Britain's Prime Minister Neville Chamberlain announced a state of war with Germany. While in no way hesitant in her duty, Canada was determined not to go to war under Britain's declaration. Parliament was assembled and on September 10 formally committed the country to the conflict. Mobilization was announced and the call for volunteers went forth. Several young men from Cornwall who had militia training with the P.E.I. Light Horse were the first to answer the call to colours; before Christmas 1939, some of them were in England with the First Canadian Division.

To Vernon and his friends, working for low wages or unemployed, Canada's call for troops offered a way out of a situation with no future. At more than a dollar a day, the pay was attractive, considering that food and clothing were supplied. The possibility of being killed or wounded on some foreign battlefield was too remote even to worry about. One by one, motivated as much by economics as patriotism, the lads started to join up.

Life as an infantry soldier held little appeal for Vernon and his buddies. The Air Force seemed a glamorous alternative to foot slogging, especially to Dan MacArthur, principal of Cornwall's two-room school. Dan had enlisted in the army in World War I, although he had not served overseas. He had a military bearing and military interests: around Cornwall he was regarded as an old soldier. His son Charles (Charlie) was about Vernon's age, and Vernon's good friend. Charlie had completed High School but had no job. Luther Horne, another of Vernon's and Charlie's friends, was a clerk in the local general store. In addition to serving the customers, Luther also on occasion tended the three-line switchboard at the telephone "Central" in the store owner's home.

Convinced that the Air Force was the service to join, Dan took Charlie, Luther and Vernon to Dartmouth, Nova Scotia to enlist. On their first day there, Charlie and Luther were interviewed by an Air Force recruiting officer and were provisionally accepted into the junior service. Vernon backed away from joining the Air Force; his choice was the Navy. He thought that he would like the sea and that the Navy would be a great way to see the world. Besides that, everyone said that Navy food was really good. His only problem was that he did not have the slightest idea how one joined the Navy.

That was a problem for tomorrow, if indeed, it was a problem at all. Was not Halifax a Naval port and would there not be sailors on the streets who would be only too willing to tell him how to join them? Meanwhile, there was an immediate problem - where to spend the night? In their enthusiasm to see the recruiting officer, they had neglected to book rooms. By the evening, accommodation was at a premium. Someone directed them to an inn of dubious quality, where they were bitten by bedbugs during the night, but to young lads this was more of a laugh than a concern. A bottle of cheap wine in a flop house was as good to them as champagne in a three-star hotel. Not for Dan, though, whose more fastidious tastes and tender anatomy were violated by the bedbugs.

Next day, wounded by vermin and suffering slightly from the after effects of the wine, the little party of Islanders crossed the harbour to Halifax. There in a book store they found two sailors, in full uniform and with "H.M.C.S. *Skeena*" on their cap ribbons. When Vernon enquired of them how he might join the Navy, neither of them showed quite the enthusiasm he had expected of persons being offered his help. On the contrary, they definitely gave the impression that anyone not in the Navy was infinitely better off than themselves, and could only be deranged in wanting to change that state. On further pressing, they finally allowed that, if Vernon was bent on his own ruin, he could accompany them back to the Dockyard where *Skeena* was alongside. They walked Vernon into the Dockyard by the old North Gate. Striding along, they smartly saluted every bit of gold braid which crossed their path, to Vernon's mounting bewilderment. They left him at the building known as the old quarterdeck, telling him to enter and he would be taken care of. Inside Vernon met someone who, in response to his request to join, went off and fetched an officer - of what rank, of course, Vernon was quite ignorant. The officer took particulars of Vernon's age, place of residence, etc., and arranged for a medical examination that very afternoon.

Vernon passed his medical and was told to go home and await a call. He was warned not to be too anxious, as there were a lot of names ahead of his - 2000 or more - but as the need arose, he would be called. The actual situation was that at this juncture the RCN had not recovered from the parliamentary neglect of the previous two decades. The influx of volunteers far exceeded the Navy's resources for training them. There was a shortage of instructors, a shortage of equipment, a shortage of facilities and a shortage of ships. At the outbreak of war, the Royal Canadian Navy had twelve ships: six River-class destroyers: HMCS *Saguenay, Skeena, Fraser, St. Laurent, Restigouche* and *Ottawa (Assiniboine* was added later in 1939); four coal-burning minesweepers; and two other vessels. There were 1700 officers and men of the Permanent Force and somewhat fewer Reservists to crew these ships and to man the shore establishments at Halifax on the east coast and Esquimalt on the west coast[1]. There were only a few experienced instructors to train new recruits and not a lot of ships in which to take them to sea. Recruits just had to wait until the Navy could absorb them.

A series of disasters in 1940 did not help the manpower situation. On June 20, 1940 HMCS *Fraser* sank after colliding with HMS *Calcutta*, with the loss of forty-seven men. On September 8 HMCS *Margaree* went down after a collision with a merchant ship in a five-ship convoy she was escorting westward from Londonderry; 142 lives were lost. Then, on December 1, twenty-one more were killed when HMCS *Saguenay* was torpedoed by the Italian submarine *Argo*. Many of these more than 200 casualties were the Navy's most experienced sailors.

True to its word, the Navy kept Vernon informed of his movement up the waiting list, but meanwhile others were entering the Navy through the Charlottetown Naval Barracks, HMCS *Queen Charlotte*. Harvey MacLean and Murchison Gordon, both of them Vernon's friends, had joined and left the Island. Vernon was getting anxious that he might be passed over; he had to do something to speed things up.

On July 2, 1940 he revolunteered at *Queen Charlotte*, then located in the Simms Building at the corner of Kent and Hillsborough streets. Lieutenant-Commander Ken Birtwhistle was the Commanding Officer at that time, and it was he who explained to Vernon the difference between the RCN (the "real Navy") and the RCNVR, the Royal Canadian Naval Volunteer Reserve. The Voluntary Reserve was the creation of Commodore Walter Hose, RCN, who organized two Divisions in Montreal in 1924. By 1939 the strength of the "VR" was 113 officers and 1292 other ranks in seventeen Divisions across the country[2]. By war's end Volunteer Reservists would make up about ninety percent of total navy enlistment, and war historians would credit the foresight of Commodore Hose for the success of Canada's naval contribution in World War II.

None of this was part of Lt. Cdr. Birtwhistle's conversation with Vernon. Much more to the point he explained that, if one chose the RCN, the enlistment was for seven years (the so-called "short service engagement" lately approved by the Admiralty); joining the Volunteer Reserve was for the duration of hostilities only and "for such period of time as His Majesty might require". Since a war lasting seven years was inconceivable, the clear choice was the RCNVR, and Vernon was duly enlisted as No. V1337. Part-time training, two evenings per week, began immediately. The call to report for service in the RCN came September 18, 1940; by then Vernon was already six weeks in the Wavy Navy[*].

There was a pending urgent matter which Vernon had to take care of; he had not informed his parents of his enlistment. When part-time training gave way to full time instruction he could no longer put off the difficult task of breaking the news to his mother and father. Their reactions were much as he expected. His mother was distraught and tearful; his father resigned, silent and pessimistic. Both of them had memories of the First World War and of the tragedies that flowed from it, and being older, they did not share youth's conviction of invincibility. But they recognized the inevitability of what had happened and under their sadness and apprehension there was pride in their son for the choice he had made. What dangers he would face, and how long he would be away were questions that no one could answer. But with all of continental Europe now under Nazi occupation, and with the outcome of the just-joined Battle of Britain uncertain, prospects of a short war had vanished.

There was no accommodation in the Charlottetown naval barracks for the full time trainees, who had to be billeted in nearby rooming houses. Without uniforms and gear, the recruits did parade square training each day, learning to stand at attention, to stand at ease, to stand easy; to march in step and to perform squad movements in unison and in correct time - "by numbers and don't rush it!". With old rifles they were put through the Manual of Arms: order arms; slope arms; shoulder arms; present arms, and so on. Instructions and orders alike were issued in stentorian tones, frequently with profane embellishments and scornful appraisals of the recruits' intelligence. It was the good old "bullshit and gaiters" served up by generation after generation of leather-lunged naval parade square instructors. Its object was to inculcate smartness, which it did, but it had a far more important outcome: the bonding of a disparate group, through shared miseries, into a functional unit. Ships' crews are built that way, too.

In the intervals between "square bashing" the recruits attended introductory classes on visual signalling (semaphore and Morse code with the Aldis lamp) and other naval skills. They also had some initiation into their new world to come, because even shore establishments were ships as far as the Navy was concerned - "stone frigates" was one name given to Naval barracks. In this new world familiar things had unfamiliar names. They themselves were called rat-

---

* The RCNVR was familiarly known as "The Wavy Navy" because its officers' gold braid insignia of rank were "zigzagged" around the sleeve cuffs of their uniforms in contrast to the straight bands worn by Regular Force officers.

ings. Their living quarters were called messes (although kept scrupulously tidy); floors were decks; walls were bulkheads. The kitchen was the galley, the bathroom the heads. And there were new names for new things: a ship's front end was the bow; the back end the stern. The right side, facing forward, was starboard, the left side, port. The forward part of a ship, where the messes were usually located, was the forecastle, or fo'c'sle; the after part was the quarterdeck. The quarterdeck was officer territory, where ratings went only when required by duty. The officers' communal living space, where ratings never went, was the wardroom.

They received instruction in rank structure, to make sense of all the saluting Vernon had seen in Halifax. Commissioned ranks were, in order of seniority, Sub-Lieutenant, Lieutenant, Lieutenant-Commander, Commander and Captain (time enough later to learn the Flag ranks, as the various grades of admiral were called). All these types merited salutes; the recruits were taught how:

*The naval salute is made by bringing up the right hand to the*
*cap, naturally and smartly, but not hurriedly, with the thumb and fin-*
*gers closed together, elbow in line with the shoulder, hands and fore-*
*arm in line, with the palm of the hand turned to the left, but inclined*
*slightly inward.[3]*

And they were taught when, and under what circumstances, to salute, including the correct protocol if riding a bicycle. The Navy thought of everything!

Non-commissioned ranks were Ordinary Seaman (where recruits started), Able Seaman, Leading Seaman, Petty Officer and Chief Petty Officer. Recruits soon learned that, while they might get by with superficial respect and a salute for an officer, genuine respect, tinged with awe, would characterize their relations with their non-commissioned superiors, especially Petty Officers and Chiefs. It mattered not that they did not merit salutes; with their experience and expertise, they were "The Navy", whom only the foolish, to their bitter chagrin, would ignore or disobey.

The Navy had its own system of reckoning time, running on a 24hr-clock, on which the hours were designated by hundreds, from one to twenty-four. On the Navy clock, 1am was 0100, 2am 0200, and so on until noon, 1200; 1pm was 1300, and so on until midnight, which was 2400. Within each hour the minutes were counted from one to fifty-nine. Thus, 9:30am was 0930, 1:20pm, 1320. One minute past midnight was 0001. A ship's day was divided into "watches" of four hours duration, beginning with first watch, from 2000 to 2400, followed by the middle, morning, forenoon, afternoon and dog watches. Passage of time within a watch was marked by "bells", eight to a watch, i.e., a bell every half-hour, from one bell to eight bells, which ended the watch. The half-hours were struck on the ship's highly polished brass bell.

For routine operation of a ship its crew was divided into groups so that some could rest while the others worked. As a further confusion to the newcomers, these groups were also called "watches". When a crew was divided into two watches, the watches were designated "starboard " and "port". Some ships operated on a three-watch system, the watches being designated "red", "white" and "blue". At sea, in a two-watch system, men worked "watch and watch"; that is, fours hours duty and four hours rest. In a three-watch system men did "four on and eight off"; that is, four hours duty and eight hours rest. In a day that had six watches of equal length, a rating would always work the same "shift" day in and day out. Seafarers had recognized this as a problem a long time ago, and solved it by inventing the dog watches. The watch from 1600 to 2000 was split into two, two-hour watches: the first dog watch and the last dog watch, thus creating seven rather than six watches in twenty-four hours. By this means a sailor's period of duty was advanced by one watch each day.

While the recruits were absorbing all this information, and more, the time was fast approaching when they would be drafted to Halifax for more thorough training. The departure date was set for October 2, 1940. It was a sombre autumn morning when the small company of Island VR's assembled at the train station in Charlottetown. The Salvation Army was there, with treats and "ditty Bags" for the boys - little gifts of candy, sewing materials, post cards, etc.. Some parents were present; Vernon's were not. Farewells had been said at home the previous night. A new feeling of loneliness pervaded the farm at Meadow Bank.

Someone had contributed a short item to the day's *Guardian* newspaper. Vernon was not mentioned but his roommate from billets was:

> *JOIN NAVY - Harris Sinclair MacFadyen, only son of Mr. and Mrs. N. D. MacFadyen of Churchill, his second cousin Burton Allen, son of Mr. and Mrs. Duncan Allen, Riverdale, leave this morning with the boys of the R.C.N.V.R. for overseas duty. It is interesting to know that Burton Allen's father served for 36 months in the first Great War in France and he is proud to have his son serve his King and country. These two lads were the first to offer their services from their school district and they are followed by the good wishes of all.*

Vernon recalls little of the train trip to Halifax, or of being met and taken to barracks. He used the first of the Salvation Army's postcards somewhere on the journey to write to his mother, "This far just fine. We have to stay on the train but don't know how long. Having a good time." In retrospect Vernon thinks it was a quiet trip because it was the first time many of them (most still in their teens) had been away from home. He and his companions had not yet learned any of the countless ways in which travelling sailors could have "fun".

In Halifax another, much larger, stone frigate awaited the Island draft: HMCS *Stadacona*, or "Stad" for short. Two more postcards left Stad on October 7. To his little brother Vernon wrote, "There are 750 in the room where I sleep. There is sure some rush when you get up in the morning". To his parents he explained, "I have not got time to write. We are very busy. I will get a letter home soon and tell you as much as I can." That could be virtually anything he chose to tell, for he usually wrote from the YMCA or the Salvation Army rooms, both beyond the censor's prying eye. In fact, his letters would have revealed nothing of value to an enemy spy, should they have been seen by one; they carefully followed the "I am well, hope you are the same" theme, augmented by his comments on the news in the latest letter from home. Once settled in, and for the duration of his service, Vernon was a faithful correspondent.

The recruits were busy, indeed. At Stad Vernon would complete his eight-week entry training in drill, dress and discipline. Each day began with "P. T." (physical training), followed by breakfast, Morning Divisions, classes and square bashing. The intervals between each activity were minimal. The first priority, however, was getting kitted out, a whole new experience for a soon-to-be tar. Standard kit was two of almost everything from the skin out: underwear, socks, sweaters, trousers, jumpers and caps; a pair of boots; a pair of sneakers; a greatcoat; an oilskin slicker; a kitbag and a hammock and blankets.

A naval rating's uniform of those days was a unique fashion, unlike any part of a civilian's wardrobe. Not only did a novice need instruction in just getting into it; he required an extensive indoctrination into the traditions behind each piece of the ensemble.

A sailor's uniform was made of a heavy wool serge in dark navy blue - a blue so deep as to be almost black. The trousers were bell-bottomed, high waisted and with a flap fly across the top. The only pocket was an inside pouch accessible by the fly. A wide web belt with a small compartment for money or small items held the trousers up. The uniform did not include a shirt, as such. In summer a sailor wore a white crew-necked singlet of flannel or cotton edged with blue jean tape, and in winter a dark blue crew-necked woollen sweater. A snugly fitting jumper took the place of a coat; it had no buttons and was pulled on over the head. Although the jumper had a square serge collar permanently attached, the uniform required an outer square jean collar, royal blue with three white stripes, worn over the jumper collar. The trick was, however, that this collar had to be put on and tied in place with its drawstrings before the jumper could be hauled on. There were two "accessories": a black silk scarf called, simply, the silk, folded upon itself several times to form a band two inches wide; and a white lanyard. Silk and lanyard were worn under the collar and brought round to the front. The ends of the silk were crossed and tied to the "V" of the jumper by a bow knot in a pair of tapes attached to the jumper. The lanyard was shortened so as to cross in front of the white flannel, the free end being tucked inside the jumper.

This unique style of dress reflected myth and tradition. Sailors of bygone days wore their hair in pigtails, which were said to be tarred; it was alleged that the collar was originally to protect the sailor's jacket from this rather strong pomade. The three white stripes on the collar were said to commemorate Admiral Lord Nelson's three great victories: Copenhagen, The Nile and Trafalgar. Another school of thought held them to be merely decorative.

The silk scarf may have served originally as a kerchief, sweatband or handwipe; new recruits were told that it was a sign of mourning for Nelson's death at Trafalgar. The lanyard was once a suspensor for a seaman's knife, but in current dress was purely decorative. Trousers were bell-bottomed so as to be more easily rolled up to be kept dry when decks had to be swabbed. For storage, the trouser legs were folded seven times; the seven creases, often laboriously ironed into the cloth, were supposed to represent the seven seas.

One of the two caps was white for summer wear in temperate latitudes and for year-round use in the tropics; the other one was blue for winter use. (After accumulating some sea time, sailors frequently wore only their blue caps, and discarded their lanyards as marks of their "saltiness".) A silk ribbon or "tally" was tied around the rim of the cap; in peace time the name of the sailor's ship was embroidered on the tally in gold letters, but in wartime the tally simply bore the letters *H.M.C.S.*, so as not to reveal the name of the ships in port.

Regulations specified the size and position of the bow by which the ribbon was tied; indeed, the wearing of all parts of the uniform was bound by regulations. In the new vernacular that Vernon was learning these regulations defined what was "pussers". Anything that was issued from naval stores, anything that was bound by naval decree, was "pussers". Any modification in uniform was termed "tiddlying" and, strictly speaking, was forbidden. In actual practice, however, a blind eye was turned to all but the most outrageous of alterations. So it would be that sooner or later a dress uniform of finer serge, tailor made to fit skin tight, would be purchased. Its trousers would be more bell-bottomed than pussers trousers, its jumper tapes longer than regulation tapes. In every group of sailors would be someone who could tie cap ribbons in very fancy, very tiddly bows placed, not over the left ear as regulations required, but well forward on the cap where it could be admired.

Then there was the hammock - two hammocks, actually, because two covers were issued - with one set of blankets and slinging apparatus: lanyard, lashing, clews and nettles. Sailors had slept in hammocks since long before Nelson's time. Hammocks saved space in crowded mess decks; they afforded a stable sleeping berth in a rolling, pitching ship; and during action in the old wooden warships they could be stacked in netting along the bulwarks as splinter shields. With the hammock, in addition to the new vocabulary of clews, nettles, etc., came a rigid set of instructions on slinging, lashing and stowing. There were also specific instructions for marking hammock, bedding and all personal gear with the owner's name; the *Manual of Seamanship* specified the size, colour and position of the identifying marks on each item of gear.

It was a lot to absorb and time was short, but young minds were keen. Besides mastering the three "D's" - drill, dress and discipline - new entrants had to choose a naval trade. Vernon chose gunnery, more or less at random, and received training as a seaman gunner. Gunnery training included generous additional portions of bullshit and gaiters, in the form of squad drill; land fighting; and operating guns as a member of a gun crew. The gunnery school at that time had one example of each principal kind of gun used by the Navy and in theory, at least, gunnery ratings received practice on each one, studying its mechanics, its mounting and its firing routine. The demands on these practice guns was so great, however, that initial training was usually sketchy, real training being left for later "on the job" after drafting to a ship.

Not all Vernon's mates were so fortunate in being assigned to the trade of their choice. One friend who opted for shipwright (carpenter/blacksmith) was made a cook, an assignment that did not bode well for the quality of naval cuisine!

While receiving instruction in his chosen trade, Vernon also had lessons to learn in seamanship. There were classes in knots and splices: reef knots, half hitches, bowlines and sheepshank; short splices, long splices, eye splices, crowns and monkey's fists - new names and new skills for these boys-not-yet-sailors to learn. A lifetime later, with years of sea time to his credit, all this and much more remains an integral part of Vernon's vocabulary and ability. He cannot now remember learning it, or who taught it to him, but learn it he had to do because none of it was part of his pre-Navy life.

Small boat work - rowing, or "pulling" as the Navy called it -was fun, but it was strenuous work in the chill autumn air over Halifax harbour and the Northwest Arm. Like everything else, pulling had to be done the Navy way. It was not enough just to sit in the boat - a 27-foot whaler or a 32-foot cutter - and pull on an oar. First there was the detail of having all the boat's crew pulling together, in unison. Then there was a new lexicon of small boat terms and their peculiar pronunciation: thwart ("th'ort") and gunwhale ("gunnel"); fore sheets and stern sheets (nothing to do with bedding!); knees, risings and crutches. And more! Lastly there were all sorts of things done with the oars besides pulling: tossing them; kissing them; boating them. The change from landsman to seaman was not easy!

Recruits' living quarters were in the Wellington barracks, E Block, in the Dockyard. Each rating had a Station Card with his personal details: religious affiliation, entitlement to rum issue, part of the ship to which he was assigned and so on. Vernon was assigned to Red Watch and, when not on duty or in training, was free to "go ashore" as leave in town was described in Navalese. Halifax was already becoming a busy, crowded place, although the level of activity was far less than it would become in this "east coast Canadian port" as the war wore on. In that autumn of 1940 the YMCA and the Salvation Army Citadel were popular spots for sailors away from home without much money to spend. They provided reading rooms and lounges and free stationery to encourage the boys to write home. In the first weeks of training, shore leave ended at 2300, but overnight passes were obtainable later. The YMCA was a popular spot where a night's lodging was available for twenty-five cents, with a hearty breakfast for an additional quarter.

A short leave home was also possible. Late in November Vernon arrived back in Meadow Bank for five days. It was his first appearance in his uniform. He created a minor sensation when he came to the school and asked that his young brother might be excused for the rest of the day. He visited all his former civilian haunts and friends, stayed out late and slept the mornings through.

It was the custom, when a young man from the district left to join the Service, to have a farewell party for him. Vernon had left for Halifax so suddenly in October that there had been no time to organize a sendoff. This first leave was an opportunity for friends and neighbours to gather at his home, to make appropriate speeches telling of the esteem in which he was held and to express godspeed and hopes for a safe return. Vernon was presented with gifts and folks lingered through the evening, chatting and playing cards and crokinole. When they departed it was with a firm handshake and a good wish for Vernon. In no time at all the brief leave was over, and the pangs of parting were felt afresh. A little account of the farewell party appeared in the *Guardian* a some days later:

*FAREWELL PARTY - A most pleasant evening was spent at Meadow Bank, West River, on the night of November 28th last when members of the Young People's Union and the Women's Institute met at the home of Mr. and Mrs. Lem Drake to pay a parting tribute of respect to their son Vernon who is with the RCNVR. The address of the Y.P.U. was read by Miss Florence MacRae at the conclusion of which a valuable set consisting of a pen and pencil was presented to seaman Drake. The address on behalf of the Women's Institute was read by Miss Laura Crosby and this organization presented Mr. Drake with a ring emblematic of the service of which he is a member.*

Vernon and his mates in *Stadacona* could look from their windows to the shipyard where a large vessel, the *Prince David*, was undergoing conversion from passenger liner to man-of-war. There were persistent rumours among the ratings in E Block that they would be *Prince David's* crew when she went to sea. Meanwhile, training continued: parade square every morning, seamanship and gunnery classes throughout the day, duty watch or shore leave in the evening. Then, just at Christmas, disaster struck E Block. Fire swept through the barrack block, destroying everything.

Fortunately, all the occupants escaped unharmed. On Boxing Day Vernon sent a cryptic telegram (collect, because even his money was gone), "Lost everything but safe love". No word of the fire had yet reached Prince Edward Island, so his parents were mystified and apprehensive until they received an explanatory letter.

New kit was immediately issued to the former residents of E Block. Added to the replacements for what was lost in the fire were uniforms of white duck - tropical gear. Something must be up, thought Vernon.

Something was up. On December 27, 1940 Ordinary Seaman Vernon Drake moved his new kit and hammock into the Canadian Armed Merchant Cruiser HMCS *Prince David*. Rumour had matured into fact; the ratings of E Block, plus others, had been drafted to that big ship in the yard. Immediately they were put to work provisioning their ship. Long lines of men formed along a wide gangway from the dock to the ship, passing to one another the flour, sugar, tea, bacon, beef, cases of tinned goods and the myriad other commodities which would be their food on the voyage to come. HMCS *Prince David* was commissioned on December 28; her captain was Commander W.B. Armit RCNR, her last peacetime skipper when she was in the Canadian National Steamships service. Harris MacFadyen, Vernon's buddy from first entry, was not with the crew of almost 400. During provisioning he had dropped a box of frozen meat on his foot and he was in hospital. But many others of the draft from Charlottetown were on board, including Reigh MacLean, a schoolmate from Meadow Bank, who was an Officer's Steward.

HMCS *Prince David* was one of "The Princes Three", as Fraser M. McKee called them[4]. The other two Princes were *Prince Henry* and *Prince Robert*. They were small luxury liners ordered for Canadian National Steamships by Sir Henry Thornton in 1929. Built in the Cammell Laird yards in Birkenhead, England, at a cost of more two million dollars each, they were delivered to the west coast of Canada in the summer of 1930 and put to work in the Vancouver - Victoria - Seattle service and on Vancouver - Alaska cruises. They could carry 334 First Class passengers and seventy Third Class passengers, with additional space for cargo, including automobiles. But the 1930s were not the best of times for passenger ships, and the Princes had varied careers, with intervals of idleness and neglect, on both coasts, before war came.

*Prince David* was launched on February 12 1930. Like her two sister ships, she was high, with a flaring bow, 385 feet long, fifty-seven feet in the beam, displacing 5,579 tons; she drew sixteen feet six inches. Her twin screws were driven by the latest Parsons turbines which could produce 14,500 shaft horsepower at 275 rpm, power enough to drive her at a top speed of 22.25 knots in her trials. As events would show, she could make that speed, or better, more than a decade later when valour (or discretion, which is the better part of valour!) demanded.

The Navy had had its eye on the three "Princes" for some time before the war, as possible additions to the fleet in a war crisis. The *David* was acquired in January 1940 for $700,000, and was sent to the Halifax shipyard on February 9. Completion of her conversion to AMC (Armed Merchant Cruiser) was scheduled for August, but her hull and machinery were in worse repair than anticipated, hence her presence in the shipyard while Vernon and his mates completed their entry-level training at *Stadacona*. The plans for *David's* conversion to AMC were drawn by Messrs. Lambert, German and Milne of Montreal, and they called for radical changes to the ship. The two top decks were removed, to be replaced by a light cruiser style superstructure. The hull and decks were strengthened, but only a minimum of watertight compartments were built into her large internal spaces, leaving her with a fundamental flaw as a warship: open access compartments extending across the hull below decks; and an undivided engine room. Her chances of surviving a torpedo hit or moderate shellfire were practically nil.

Her major armament was four 6-inch guns in single mounts, two forward and two aft. The guns had been manufactured in 1896 as secondary firepower in *King Edward*-class battleships of the Royal Navy. Their age and design posed considerable difficulties in their effective use, as will be noted later. *Prince David's* secondary armament was, by comparison, quite modern: two 3-inch guns, designed in 1916 for use on light cruisers. Twin Vickers machine guns mounted on each wing of the bridge, and a pair of depth charge chutes at the stern completed her offensive weaponry. She had no ASDIC (submarine detection) equipment and no radar. Range finding and fire control of her guns could best be described as rudimentary. An experienced naval person, inspecting this ship, might have been reminded of Wellington's characterization of the reinforcements sent to him in Portugal: "I do not know whether they frighten the enemy, but by

God, Sir, they frighten me!" But *Prince David* and the other two Princes were the largest warships in the RCN then and for several years after, and to her unsalted crew she looked large enough and powerful enough to take on anything in the German Navy.

A day or two after commissioning, having been provisioned, ammunitioned and fuelled, *Prince David* was in the Bedford Basin "swinging ship". The magnetic compass was still the principal navigational device in 1940. While in theory the compass needle always points to the earth's north magnetic pole, in practice, in a steel ship, the compass magnets are diverted from the true magnetic north by the attraction of the ship's metal. Before going to sea, this deviation as it is called had to be determined by reading the compass while ranging the ship on known bearings. The differences between the compass readings and the true bearings were recorded and tabulated for the navigator's later use at sea.

When all the necessary readings had been taken, the ship returned through the Narrows towards her berth at the dockyard jetty, but when she was within heaving line distance of the jetty she veered off into the fairway, gathered speed down the harbour and passed the gate into the Atlantic. McNab's Island and Hangman's Beach passed on the port side, the long guns of York Redoubt on the starboard. It would be the better part of nine months before anyone on board would see these landmarks again. Ahead, a storm-bothered Atlantic thrashed and roiled. *Prince David's* wartime service, and with it Vernon's life at sea, had begun.

1.  D. Hannington VII. 75 Years of Service. The rise of the Canadian Navy" in Wings magazine Commemorative Issue, (Calgary: Corvus Publishing Group, 1985), 20 - 34.

2.  Ibid.

3.  *Manual of Seamanship*. (Ottawa: King's Printer, 1942), 7.

4.  Fraser M. McKee, "Princes Three: Canada's Use of Armed Merchant Cruisers in World War II" in *RCN In Retrospect*, ed. by James A. Boutilier. Ch 8.

## 2. GOING TO SEA: A WHIFF OF SALT AND TAR.

Whatever the signals sent and received that afternoon, *Prince David* was clearly not "in all respects ready for sea". There was a lot of gear, including hawsers and wires, unsecured on deck; the lifeboats did not have their gripes in position; Carley floats were not secure. The wind was already up and a storm was brewing; it was a rough start for a green crew. Green in more ways than one, for seasickness soon took its toll among these landsmen in Navy uniforms, three-quarters of whom had never seen the ocean before. Not everyone succumbed. One fellow who worried greatly before going to sea was unaffected; Vernon himself, although feeling the effects of the ship's motion, quickly got his sea legs, and kept all his meals where they properly belonged.

The first care was to secure as much of the loose gear as possible, and the young sailors worked hard at their unfamiliar tasks. But the heightening waves were soon breaking over the exposed deck and flooding into the open hatches; the hatches were closed, the hands ordered to shelter, and the rest of the unsecured gear left to wash over the side.

The storm continued unabated the next day. The duty watches huddled miserably on deck, seeking protection from wind and water behind gun shields or other shelters. From one such spot, Vernon and Able Seaman Zienck, an old hand who had sailed on square riggers, spied an inbound three master, heeled hard over, flying through clouds of spray; with an envious oath, Zienck wished himself aboard of her instead of in the *David*. For they were quickly getting to know one of the *David's* less endearing qualities: her propensity to roll in a peculiarly jerky way. Whether because of her original design, or because of the changes in her due to conversion, she was notorious for her roll. The seaman's messes were forward; it was not the best of locations, for the ship was somewhat wet when facing heavy seas. In a head sea, Prince David would bury her fore-castle in green water which before long found the cracks and crevices where leaks intruded. But the mess decks were spacious and otherwise comfortable; in fact there were unused spaces in the ship, unheard of in a man-o'-war.

No landsman can imagine the vastness of the sea. Only a seafaring man can comprehend the ocean's size and its wild swings of mood from sunlit tranquility to black crashing fury. Over the decade that Vernon would spend at sea that vastness and those shifts of mood would become as familiar to him as the farm fields, the summer rains and the winter snows he had left behind in Prince Edward Island. In his years in the Navy and the Merchant Marine, Vernon came to know the sea as only a sailor can, gleaning from this intimate knowledge a treasure of memories so rich that even now he finds it incredible that there was a time when he knew nothing of the sea; a time when he did not even know its colour. He soon learned that "the deep blue sea" belongs more to the realm of poetry than to reality. Blue the sea could be, for sure, but more often it was green, or grey, or even black.

Before he left the land he had imagined the sea as an empty place. He knew intuitively that fish were there, and he was not surprised by the gulls following his ship to sea and meeting it on its approach to land. Gulls are coastal birds, their range a hundred miles or so, as they ride the air currents on their precisely set pinions, alert for any scrap of garbage tossed over a ship's side. But he was not prepared to find, far offshore, delicate little dark birds skimming the wavetops and seeming never to alight on the water. "Mother Carey's chickens" the older sailors called them; in bird books they are "Leach's Petrels", but few sailors read bird books.

Vernon thought (and hoped) that he would see whales, the large whales of his imagination. On occasion he did. What he did not expect (and what caused him endless pleasure to observe) were those smaller whales - dolphins - leaping and frolicing in the ship's spreading bow wave; on rare sunbright afternoons they would race with the ship for hours on end.

Sharks, too, were on Vernon's list of expected sea creatures, more to be feared than to be enjoyed. When an opportunity presented, usually in harbour, Vernon and others would fish over the ship's side for shark with baited meat hooks on heaving lines.* Occasionally they would haul a thrashing captive victim on deck. As to species, the sailors were largely indifferent; a shark to them was a shark, and the best shark was a dead one. Vernon's souvenirs of the sea include several triangular, keen-edged white teeth extracted from captured sharks.

The least expected of all sea phenomena was what, for want of a better word, Vernon called phosphorescence. On certain nights at sea, water breaking away from the ship's side, or bubbling up in the wake, shone with a pale glow. Biologists call this condition "bioluminescence" (light produced by living things) and it is far more common in the ocean than Vernon realized. The light which he and his shipmates observed is produced mostly by tiny marine organisms living near the surface of shallow coastal waters. When disturbed by the passage of a ship each little creature emits a brief flash of pale greenish light. The cumulative effect of countless such flashes is to make the water glow, to the utter amazement of novice sailors. Vernon chuckles when telling of a conscientious young officer, seeing bioluminescence for the first time, being convinced that, because of someone's carelessness, the ship was not properly darkened. In his innocence he even called out the watch to find the open scuttle or unshaded light causing the illumination.

When pressed, Vernon can recall moonlit nights of gentle calm and splendid days when the ocean breathed easily under flawless skies; days when flying fish broke surface to scud across the low swells; days when his ship was centred in sun-dappled water while all around her the horizon was studded with black pillars of tropical rain showers. But the memories that come most readily to his mind are of the storms: not just the run-of-the-mill high winds, but the real big storms - Atlantic gales; their oft-time parents, Caribbean hurricanes; and Pacific typhoons. In his life at sea, Vernon met them all. And the ships in which he sailed

---

* A light, weighted rope, thrown from ship to jetty when a ship is coming alongside. Its inboard end is tied to a heavy hawser, which can be hauled ashore and secured to a bollard.

weathered them all, although not always without damage, and never without travail.

Only personal experience can give the real measure of a storm at sea - its "immeasurable, incomparable force and fury", as James Lamb[1] has described it. Vernon soon appreciated that neither ship nor seaman conquers storm or rules the waves. At best they survive forces incalculably greater than their own.

The first hint of an impending storm is what sailors call a falling glass, by which they mean lowering atmospheric pressure as measured on the ship's barometer. But in a way they cannot explain, old salts can sense the coming fury before the barometer forecasts its imminence. They say they can "sniff it in the wind", but they are probably reacting to the first subtle changes in air pressure and to barely tangible alterations in wind and sea. Less experienced sailors read their future in later, more patent signs: halyards standing out more stiffly; ensign snapping more briskly; the rising wind keening past aerials and standing rigging at a higher pitch; and the ship responding to the stirring seas with a livelier motion. Ships have two basic responses to seas: side-to-side movement, or rolling; and up-and-down movement, or pitching. Depending on wind and sea directions, her course and her sea-keeping qualities, a ship's movements will be predominantly pitch, roll or some combination of the two.

In a gathering storm the roaring wind shreds the crests of the growing waves into white lancets of stinging spray which lash the sailors. Great, towering seas build up around the ship, seeming to elbow one another to get at her. Higher and higher they rise, to thirty, forty, fifty feet or higher. The howling gale tears at ship and crew as the ship bores on against these monstrous seas. As steeply as the ship climbs one side of a wave, so sharply does she descend on the other side, into a deep trough where, for a breathless instant, she wallows, straining to rise on the wave poised above her. Then, as the bow begins to come up, the wave crashes down in tons of wild water. The ship shudders and writhes like a living thing. While the crest of the wave races over her, the base of the monster continues under her. The ship rises, shrugging off the tons of green which depart with bad grace, sweeping the decks in cold rage, crashing into gun shields, superstructure, boats, railings, stanchions and ventilators; hammering, snarling, hissing, seeking to tear and smash and clear everything before them. And then, having attained the summit of a heaving comber the ship slides down its sloping side to crash in the next trough.

On the open bridge officers and men wedged in corners, clinging to whatever support they can find, must somehow endure to maintain control of the ship. Gale-flung spray lashes faces and probes oilskins, finding crevices lost to anything else, wetting and chilling tired bodies. Much of the watch's work on deck is suspended. The steeply slanting, flooded decks are unsafe. If a man must move on them, he must hold fast to a lifeline while making a dash between rushes of water. It is safer to be below, even if there it is all noise and motion and stale air. All the scuttles are closed, the deadlights dogged down, doors and hatches shut. Movement is possible, but it is a lurching, uncertain movement, steadied by handholds and timed to the rolling and pitching of the ship. Sea legs mean little in conditions like these. Lucky the watch that can sling their hammocks; at least the "micks" are relatively stable. Crockery is at risk, meals are barely manageable. A fanny of kye - that thick, warm rich cocoa drink which has sustained the Navy through many a long and tiresome watch - may once again work its restorative magic on weary men waiting out the weather's anger, if it can be brought forward from the galley.

In the ceaseless clamour of the storm, water finds its way into the ship, to slosh across the decks with each change of angle. Waves as solid as walls of stone batter hull and upperworks, bending and occasionally even carrying away armoured steel. The officer of the watch eases the ship's ordeal as best he can by adjusting course and speed; on the wheel the helmsman tries to ease the bows into the waves; at the engine telegraphs the revolutions are reduced to slow the screws when they break clear, lest in their racing they shake themselves loose. But there is only so much that can be done. Plunging, rolling, shuddering, rising, she takes her punishment and survives the hours or days until the storm abates.

Wind and waves and noise diminish. Normal watchkeeping is resumed. Damage is assessed and temporary repairs made where needed. Bruised and weary, but having been tested and not found wanting, the sailors feel a new confidence in themselves and in the durability and the reliability of their ship.

Thus does Vernon remember storms at sea. This first one, bad enough for any novice, was less fierce than many he would later endure. By the third day it had subsided. Vernon and his mates began to fall into the routine of a warship at sea. They got used to turning out for watch, and trying to sleep between watches in the "four hours on, eight hours off" three-watch system. They got used to their living quarters, where each person had a space over the mess tables to sling his hammock. They got used to the evening routine of darkening ship, with red lighting inside and no light of any colour outside to betray their presence on the sea. They got used to the lack of privacy; no person had claim to personal space except for a wooden locker in which to store his gear. They got used to the food, which was plain, but edible. The large freezers and a bakery left over from the ship's first life as a liner ensured a supply of frozen foods and the luxury of fresh bread. (In the warmer south, cockroaches infested the ship, but food swarming with insects and bread with baked-in bugs were experiences still ahead).

They got used to the Navy meal time routine. RCN ships used a system of common messing, whereby all the food was prepared in the galley and eaten in the individual messes. Some time before each meal a member of each mess (designated "Cook-of-the-Mess") went to the galley to receive the food for all his messmates. He carried the food back to his mess, oversaw its distribution and cleaned up the messware after the meal. It was a system which guaranteed that the food was never too hot to eat by the time it was served up! A "Cook" worked for one day, each member of the mess taking his turn.

They got used to the Navy ritual of grog. The daily drink, or "tot", of rum was a centuries-old Navy tradition predating Nelson's time. The original daily issue had been half a pint per man, of a spirit far more potent than modern rums, and its consumption must have gone a long way towards dulling the miseries of life in the Royal Navy under sail. Sometime in the eighteenth century Admiral Vernon (in no way my brother's namesake!) conceived the idea of diluting the daily rum drink with water. Tradition has it that Admiral Vernon was nicknamed by his sailors, "Old Grogram" because of the coat he wore; hence the watered rum he served out to them became known as grog. Be that as it may, daily grog was a fixture in the Navy that Vernon Drake joined. Its issue was not, however, automatic. A rating had to be twenty years old to receive grog, and even then he had to ask for it. Each rating's Station Card bore a notation, "G.T." or U.A.", according to whether he took grog or not. Vernon was U.A., meaning that he did not receive grog, but not necessarily meaning that he lacked for rum, as will be clear later. The designation did mean, however, a tiny increase in his pay called "grog money".

At 1100 the pipe*, "Up Spirits". was given. Ratings from each mess mustered at the rum store where, under an officer's watchful eye, the coxswain measured out from an oaken cask an appropriate volume of neat spirit for each mess. Petty Officers and Chiefs had the doubtful privilege of consuming their rum undiluted, but all other ranks were supposed to mix their issue with an equal volume of water to create `grog'. Neat or diluted, the rum was to be drunk immediately upon issue. Hoarding was not countenanced.

A future shipmate of Vernon's, fellow Islander Jack Thomson, describes his introduction to Navy rum:

> The food was terrible [on HMCS Assiniboine]. Red lead [stewed canned tomatoes] and bacon in the morning. I couldn't go the bacon; it wouldn't be cooked. It was terrible! I was 122 pounds when I went on there. Eventually, when I was twenty, I drew the rum. The old three-badger*, he says, "Draw your rum when you're twenty, and you'll eat." I'll never forget that twentieth birthday. I had a cup with the rum in it and a cup of water, and I went to pour the water into the rum, and he caught me by the arm and says, "What are you doing?" I said, "I'm putting some water in it." He says, "Look, you've been sailing for a year now. Down the hatch!" So I downed the hatch. And I never uttered another word for half an hour and I burned right to my belly button.[2]

How strictly the regulations attending the issue and consumption of grog were observed varied from ship to ship. Vernon would learn that both grog and neat rum could, by various strategems, be set aside for future use by his messmates, although it was quickly realized that the diluted product went mouldy if kept too long. In the last ship in which Vernon served (HMCS *Uganda*) an overcalculation (deliberate or innocent) in the initial assessment of his mess' entitlement assured them of an excess of neat spirit throughout their commission, and the basis of many a quiet off-watch party on the darkened fo'c'sle.

---

* Notes on the boatswain's pipe (a shrill whistle) preceded issuance of a general order. Hence, `piping'.
* Senior hand who has earned three Good Conduct badges after at least thirteen years service.

Navy rum was an important form of currency on board ship and ashore. On board, small favours could be negotiated between shipmates in return for a share of the daily grog. A system of payments, ranging from "sippers" through "gulpers" to the entire tot could arrange changes in duty assignments or purchase services such as a tying a tiddly cap bow. Another fellow Islander who would eventually sail with Vernon in HMCS *Uganda*, Joe LeClair, explains:

> *When I wasn't at Action Stations I was in the Commander's office.*
> *Me and Grogan and old Chief Gunner's Mate Nettleton. There was*
> *a Watch and Quarters Bill, you know, with every rating on the ship*
> *and when you went ashore, you'd pick a list of names. This guy*
> *would be on Shore Patrol, and this guy, and so on. You'd pick all*
> *these jobs and then you'd have to go around and notify them. Lots*
> *of times I'd go around, the guy would say, "I don't want to go ashore*
> *tonight." or, "I don't want to do Shore Patrol." He'd give me a*
> *couple ot tots to put someone else's name on it. I used to get ham-*
> *mered half the time, but that's the way it was.[3]*

Rum smuggled ashore could move minor mountains: dockyard sentries could be rendered blind to certain comings and goings; recalcitrant clerks in Naval Stores could be convinced to part with items which earlier they had sworn were unavailable. But where rum had its best rate of exchange was when berths were shared with American ships. Ships of the USN were officially "dry" and their crews would barter all manner of goods and services for a bottle of over-proof rum.[4]

These familiarities with storms and rum were to be acquired in a more distant future. The immediate future for Vernon and the rest of *Prince David's* new crew was a new destination, Bermuda, and a rendezvous with the *Prince Henry* which had sailed from Halifax just hours before the *David*. Once together, the two Princes would do training exercises ("working up", the Navy called it) in company with another AMC, HMS *Queen of Bermuda* and the battleship HMS *Duke of York*.

1. James B. Lamb, *On the Triangle Run*. (Don Mills, Ontario: Collins    Paperbacks, 1989)

2. Recorded conversation with ex AB Jack Thomson, March 18 2000.

3. Recorded conversation with ex AB Joe LeClair, March 20 2000.

4. Alan D. Butcher, *I Remember Haida*. (Hantsport, Nova Scotia: Lancelot Press, 1985) 23 - 24.

## 3. WORKING UP: BECOMING A CREW.

*Prince David* was no stranger to Hamilton, Bermuda. Captain Armit had taken her there in peace time. The entrance to the harbour at Hamilton is via a narrow, twisting channel between reefs of coral, and on his previous trip, Capt. Armit missed a turn in the channel and ran SS *Prince David* up onto the coral, from which he had to be hauled off by tug. On his approach in HMCS *Prince David* he again missed a turn in the channel, and once more the *David* bounced over the coral and ground to a stop. It is said that as he assessed the situation from his position on the bridge, Commander Armit was heard to say, "God damn her, she did it again!"

After being set free from the reef, the ship went into drydock for inspection of her bottom. No serious damage was found; one plate on the starboard bow was replaced, and soon the ship was refloated. But her presence in the drydock provided a wonderful opportunity for her crew to get a novel view of their ship. Down in the drydock, under her massive hull, they marvelled at her great bulk, and her huge twin screws.

Working up was a busy time. While continuing to learn the basics of seamanship, all hands had to perfect their roles at Action Stations. Seaman gunners had to be moulded into smoothly working guns' crews. Ammunition parties had to learn their tasks of serving the guns. Damage control parties had to be taught how to cope with the effects of enemy fire.

Vernon's action station was in the forward shell room, deep below decks. With one or two others, it was his job to put the 100-lb shells in bags which were hoisted up to the guns by block and tackle. It was not a place for an introspective or a claustrophobic person to be, and when the order would come to abandon ship, Vernon claimed a record time for ascending the narrow, vertical steel ladders to the upper deck. Fortunately, he made these trips only in practice, and never in the urgency of a battle gone badly.

For the gun crews there was a special set of difficulties. The six-inch guns were originally designed to train over a narrow arc ("training", in naval gunnery, is moving the gun barrel from side to side; "laying", on the other hand, is changing the elevation of the barrel). In their new mountings on *Prince David* the guns were expected to train through more than 200 degrees, from abaft the beam on one side to abaft the beam on the opposite side. The training was done by hand cranks working a cog against a large toothed wheel on the deck under the gun. At the best of times, the guns trained sluggishly, but after a few days of stormy weather, they were almost immovable; it was not unusual for most of the gun's crew to leave the gun shield and push on the barrel while the trainer strained on his cranks to bring the gun to bear.

To the best of Vernon's knowledge, no enemy was ever damaged by fire from *Prince David's* guns. On the other hand, considerable damage usually resulted in the ship herself when the six-inchers went off. Below-decks lighting would be blown out, and the vibration would rattle loose and shatter any crockery which was not secured. On *Prince Henry*, the effects were somewhat different: one night-time salvo brought on all the ship's running lights. In the confusion of trying to extinguish them, someone set off the ship's siren, which whooped lustily for some minutes.

The rudimentary nature of gunnery control is illustrated by the following story, told by Fraser McKee.[1] A tug from Bermuda was hauling a target for the gunners to aim at, towing it sufficiently far astern as to make the tug safe from an errant shell. After the first salvo from the *Henry*, four fountains of water erupted around the tug. When they had subsided the tug was still afloat, but was signalling rather urgently to the *Henry*: "Please fire at target, not at tug".

The primary purpose of working up was to make an inexperienced ship's company into an efficient, effective fighting team. In practice, it had another effect, in that it was the opportunity for each individual to decide on the wisdom of his choice in joining the Navy. (Not that there was much anyone could do upon realizing that his choice was a poor one, other than to adapt to a bad situation.) In Vernon's case, no adaptation was necessary. He quickly knew that he liked the Navy, and moreover, he knew what he wanted most to do in the routine work of a ship at sea. He wanted to be a helmsman, to steer the ship.

*One of the most important duties of a seaman is to be able to steer efficiently and well. This art can only be acquired by constant practice and careful attention to details.*[2]

Vernon was tutored in the "art" by a senior hand, Chief Petty Officer Lockhart, until he was considered experienced enough to stand his "trick" on the wheel. A trick consisted of one hour's steering; at the end of his trick, the helmsman was relieved and assumed general duties in the wheelhouse, assisting the quartermaster or the boatswain's mate, running errands for the Officer of the Watch or doing a trick in the crow's-nest.

Steering was a job that Vernon really enjoyed, and enjoying it, did very well. He quickly learned to hold the ship to her compass course, even in foul weather, partly by watching the compass closely and bringing the ship back on course when she was diverted by wind or wave or current, and partly through an almost indefinable "feel" for the movement of the ship under his feet. Even on the *David*, with a high, relatively exposed wheelhouse, the helmsman had little to look at, or to see, except the compass, either the magnetic compass in its binnacle, or as it more often was, a repeater of the gyro compass which was mounted deep in the ship. The "eyes" of the ship were the officers on the bridge, who, in a chain of command from the Officer of the Watch through the Navigator to the Captain himself, set the course, advised changes in course, and supervised the ship's headway. An elaborate protocol for receiving and executing steering orders was rigidly observed. A course change to starboard could elicit the following dialogue between the Officer of the Watch and the helmsman, conducted through a voice pipe connecting bridge and wheelhouse:

O.O.W: *"Starboard twenty!"*.

Helmsman: *"Starboard twenty, sir"*

*Then turns the ship's wheel to starboard until*

twenty degrees shows on the helm indicator in front
of him and reports,

Helm: "Twenty degrees starboard wheel on sir".
The ship is now answering to the helm, and the Officer
of the Watch is noting the bearing of the ship's head
as she swings. To check her swing he will order,

O.O.W: "Midships!"

Helm: "Midships, sir." He returns the wheel to midships
position and reports,

Helm: "Wheel's amidships, sir".
The ship's head is still swinging to starboard, and
as it approaches the new course heading the Officer
of the Watch calls,

O.O.W: "Port, ten!'

Helm: "Ten degrees port wheel on, sir.
An experienced officer will have given this order in
time to bring the ship's head as nearly as possible
stationary on the new course. He then orders.

O.O.W: "Steady!"
The helmsman has been carefully watching the compass
and when he hears the order, "Steady" he reads the com
pass bearing and calls it up to the bridge:

Helm: "Steady on 123, sir." He steadies the ship on 123 degrees
and reports to the bridge:

Helm: "Compass course 123 degrees, sir."
This could end the exchange, unless a minor adjustment
in course should be necessary.

This stylized protocol became so ingrained that when Vernon became a helmsman on a merchant ship some years later he automatically replied to his first steering order by repeating it to the officer who issued it. That officer, slightly amused, said to Vernon, "I guess you must have been in the Navy. Well we don't bother with that stuff on this ship; you get an order, you just do it!"

A good helmsman soon learned to feel changes in the ship's heading before the compass revealed them, and to correct the changes by subtle movements of the helm, so that the ship's bow was steady and her wake remained straight.

No HMC ship had radar in 1941. Probably no one in an HMC ship had even heard of it. Lookouts posted in various parts of the ship. scanning sea and sky with powerful binoculars, watched for other ships, obstacles, navigational hazards and/or the enemy. The higher a lookout was above the sea, the farther he could see. In *Prince David* the high point was the crow's-nest, a chest-deep bucket attached to the foremast some twenty-five to thirty feet above the bridge. Access to this aerie was by a vertical steel ladder, about ten inches wide, welded to the after side of the mast. To do his trick in the crow's-nest, a rating climbed this ladder until he was high enough to drop over the lip and into the bucket. In a calm sea the climb was daunting enough for some, but when the sea was up and the ship was sprightly, a trip to and from the crows'-nest provided all the thrills any sailor needed for one watch. Some ratings enjoyed the crow's-nest once they found the stomach for it and, like Jack Thomson, would "buy" a trick with a tot.

Vernon did his regular tricks aloft but his most memorable experience of the crow's-nest was an occasion when he was not in it, but on the bridge. It was a clear sunny day and the sea was empty to the far horizon. Nothing had been heard from the crow's-nest since Fred* had gone up nearly an hour previously, which was no cause for concern, considering the weather. When, however, out of a cloudless sky precipitation fell on the bridge and the officer of the watch, Vernon was sent up the mast to investigate. As soon as he peered over the rim of the bucket, the situation was obvious. Fred had taken some rum with him, the better to enjoy a warm afternoon in the serenity of the crow's-nest; after drinking his fill and responding to a call of Nature, he was settling down for an afternoon nap in his lofty perch.

Vernon was, of course, obliged to report the situation. He was given a heaving line and sent back up with orders to "get that man down". As the crow's-nest is designed for one person, Vernon had all he could do to rouse the now somnolent Fred, pass the line around him and fashion a sling by which to lower him safely to the bridge. He then had to lift him bodily out of the bucket and sway him as gently as possible to his fate. That fate was foregone: immediate confinement to the rattle (punishment cell) until sober; eventual appearance on charge before the Executive officer; and punishment.

C.P.O. Lockhart's interest in him led to Vernon having yet another duty which he greatly enjoyed. The Chief assigned Vernon as a crewman on the first motor boat, the largest and most used of *Prince David's* boats. Vernon began as sternsheetsman, to learn the routine, and later was promoted to coxswain of the boat. The coxswain ("coxen", phonetically) was steersman and in charge of the boat. The advantage of this duty was that in harbour the motor boat was often in use, freeing its crew from shipboard routine and allowing them contacts with shore denied to their pals on board.

Shore leave in Bermuda introduced Vernon and his mates to a sun-charmed world, where flowers bloomed year round; where skin colours ranged from white to black; and where gaunt horses wearing straw hats sedately pulled open carriages along narrow quiet streets, or dozed between the shafts while waiting for the next fare. The coral base of Bermudian land is innocent of fresh water aquifers; the tiled roofs of the pastel houses collected runoff from the rains to provide domestic water. The evaporators on board *Prince David* were always taxed to supply fresh water for the ship's use; when in Bermuda it seemed that the ship's water was particularly scarce. A belief persisted  below decks that the ship's officers were selling water ashore for their private profit, but there was no solid proof.

Probably few of the newcomers to the Navy in *Prince David* knew that Ireland Island, the Royal Navy establishment at Bermuda was, at the hey-day of

---

* Not his real name

22

Empire, the home base for the North American and West Indies Squadron. Fewer still, below decks or above, were cognizant that they sailed in the wakes of Royal Navy greats such as Cunningham, Beatty, Jellicoe and Fisher, or that other princes, the kind who became kings, had preceded the *Princes David* and *Henry* in these pleasant waters.

So, in the warm tropical seas, in comparative safety, and with flying fish rather than periscopes breaking the surface, the training went on. When it was considered that at least a rudimentary level of efficiency had been attained, the units of the little fleet separated. *Queen of Bermuda* and *Duke of York* resumed convoy duty; *Prince Henry* sailed for the west coast of South America to take up patrol duties, and P*rince David* remained in the Caribbean, maintaining a nominal blockade of Martinique, where suspected blockade runners were awaiting an opportunity to break out.

---

1. Fraser M. McKee, "Princes Three: Canada's Use of Armed Merchant Cruisers in World War II. at V in RCN in Retrospect, ed. by James A. Boutilier. ch 8.

Naval Fashions
a). A strictly pusser RN three-badger, all elements of dress correct, demonstrating the naval salute. *(Manual of Seamanship, Vol. I, 1942)*.
b). A rather more tiddly RCNVR Able Seaman dressed for a run ashore.

## 4. HMCS PRINCE DAVID ON OPERATIONS:
## NOT THE TERROR OF THE SEAS.

In the mid-winter months of 1941, HMCS *Prince David* patrolled along the arc of the Windward Islands, using St. Lucia as a convenient port from which to watch Martinique, and Trinidad for fuelling. There was shore leave in St. Lucia and Trinidad, and in Curacao, too, where the ship once went for oiling. New sights, new smells, new tastes, greeted them on every run ashore. In lovely Castries, where the island's steep sides plunge to the depths, the northern boys were intrigued to see women doing the hard labour of coaling ship. It took time to get accustomed to the open drains, and to the humid heat but adjusting to a surfeit of fresh fruit, as well as draughts of coconut milk, came easily. A package of cigarettes would buy an entire stalk of bananas or a bag of grapefruit. Local rums cost two shillings and sixpence the bottle, if one supplied the bottle, but such easy availability required some caution in consumption. On one occasion a friend of Vernon's accompanied him to an afternoon movie. Unknown to Vernon, his friend had a concealed flask of rum from which, during the show, he took hefty pulls through a flexible tube. At the show's end, when the lights came up, Vernon's friend was unable to rise from his seat, and had to supported all the way back to the ship.

Full uniform of white duck was shore-going rig, and it was less than comfortable in the tropical heat. In Trinidad, rather than walk, Vernon and his buddies would frequently rent a car and explore the island, with its great variety of exotic crops - bananas, citrus, sugar cane, yams, lentils, cocoa, coffee and even rubber - and its unfamiliar sights of green mountains, palm-fringed beaches and multi-hued people. At San Fernando, where the ship sometimes refuelled, they were amazed by the great pitch lake lying black and hot and yielding under the sun. Was it really bottomless, as some believed? The Yankee dollar had not yet become the preferred currency, and the boys could afford souvenirs from vendors ashore and from the bumboats alongside. Bay rum from St. Lucia and a Trinidadian cane cutter's machete were two treasures that eventually found their way back to Meadow Bank.

It was an idyllic time, but after all, there was a war to be fought.

There was the immediate matter of the blockade runners. Were they still anchored in Fort-de-France, or had they slipped away? A reconnoitre would provide the answer, but how to get past the three forts which guarded the large harbour? Enter in disguise, was the answer. Hands were put to work to conceal the guns behind canvas shields, and a sailor with sewing talents was detailed to counterfeit a Brazilian flag. The plan was, when all was ready, for *Prince David*, masquerading as a Brazilian freighter, to approach the French island base in the first light of dawn, getting in close enough to determine what ships lay in the harbour. Vernon does not recall what plans were made for withdrawal; perhaps it was the failure to solve this dilemma that led to cancellation of the mad scheme.

In the succeeding months blockading was abandoned. *Prince David* was assigned to convoy duty out of Bermuda, shepherding slow (4 - 6 knots) convoys northwards and eastward from the Caribbean. Without ASDIC*, the *David* was little use against submarines, and with her outmoded deck armament she was no match for an enemy surface raider. At best, she might keep an enemy AMC at bay, laying smoke to hide her convoy, or take a blockade runner as prize, as *Prince Robert* had done off Manzanilla the previous September[1]. As it was, she kept station in the centre of the convoys where, presumably, her presence was some small comfort to worried skippers and crews. Each daybreak, she would hare off to find the night's stragglers and chivvy them back to position.

Only once was there a tentative contact with the enemy. *Prince David* was steaming alone, closed up for action stations at dawn. The Captain was on the bridge, peering through his binoculars at an object just reported by a lookout. He called the Executive Officer to the bridge from his action station aft and, handing over his binoculars, asked of him, "Do you see that?" Through the glasses, the "X. O." could clearly see the upper masts and the rangefinding director of a large warship whose course was directly towards them. Well aware that no friendly ships were in the vicinity, the Captain enquired, "What do you think we should do?" The Executive Officer's answer was straightforward: "I don't know what you are going to do, sir, but I'm getting to hell back aft to my action station, because the first place they're going to fire at is this bridge!" A challenge in international code was sent by signal lamp to the stranger: "WHO ARE YOU?" Back came the response: "WHO ARE YOU ASKING WHO I AM?" That was enough for the Captain. With no convoy that he was obliged to protect, he was not risking his ship to the same fate as befell *Rawalpindi* and *Jervis Bay*; he turned *Prince David* around to the south and rang down to the engine room for maximum revs. Simultaneously, the other ship altered away and was soon lost to sight.

In the *David's* engine room the Chief Engineer plied oil to the boilers and steam to the turbines. The straining engines set every loose thing on board to vibrating. Vernon recalls going to the heads, which were right at the stern, and seeing the toilet seats dancing madly on their hinges. The flaring bows flung sheets of spray to the winds; the racing screws churned up a boiling, billowing wake of foaming water across the face of the sea. The ship equalled, and may even have surpassed, her best speed in trials more than a decade earlier. It was exhilarating, and it was far and away better than being shot at!

There was much speculation about this contact. What ship was it? Why had she turned away when she might have destroyed them with a single salvo? It was generally assumed that the contact was a German vessel; an American aircraft later reported a German pocket battleship in the area, but which one? A persistent belief in the *David* was that they had met the German heavy cruiser *Prinz Eugen*. If so, why had she turned away? There were two plausible hypotheses: 1), *Prince David's* conversion gave her something of the appearance of a heavy

---

* Submarine detection by underwater sound waves. Now called SONAR.

cruiser when viewed bow-on, and the German did not want to take on such an adversary; or 2), the German, for one reason or another, wished to avoid detection. For it was a given that should a British ship be engaged, whatever the immediate outcome of the action might be, she would call up every Royal Navy ship within radio range, and the German would be hounded to destruction. Without air reconnaissance one could be certain only of what was visible above the horizon; whether to maintain secrecy, or to get safely back to port, the German's best strategy was to avoid engagement.

McKee's account of the incident gives the date only as "the spring of 1941", but he names Armit as the *David's* captain, which would require that the contact had to take place prior to March 24, the last day of Armit's command.[2] Fritz-Otto Busch[3] relates that in March 1941 *Scharnhorst* and *Gneisenau* were seeking victims "on the route between North America and Great Britain". Near dusk on March 16, 1941 *Scharnhorst* received a signal from her tanker, some distance away below the horizon, "Enemy battleship sighted". Busch goes on to state that *Gneisenau*, which was standing by the tanker, was challenged. The Germans were under strict orders not to engage British warships and in Busch's words, "the half light and [a] rainstorm...allowed the battleships to escape". If, indeed, it was the *Gneisenau* that *Prince David* challenged, with *Scharnhors*t just over the horizon, Captain Armit's decision was a wise one, and *Prince David's* escape nothing short of miraculous. Martin Stephen, however, states that it was HMS *Rodney* who sighted the German battleships on March 16. Stephen does not mention a challenge.[4]

In March, Captain Armit fell from a steel ladder, breaking a leg. He had to leave the ship he had commanded in peace and war; the crew lined up to bid him farewell, and there were tears in his eyes as he was carried ashore, March 24, 1941. Next day Commander Ken Adams RCN assumed command. Adams was a good ship handler who delighted in showing off his skills to the skippers of the "Lady" ships and the American Fruit Line ships in Caribbean ports. Crews took pride, too, in a captain who could handle a ship well, and under Adams' command morale in the lower decks improved.

Spring gave way to summer as convoy succeeded convoy without incident. In May Vernon was rated Able Seaman, the Navy's certification that he could now be entrusted to do a sailor's work with minimal supervision. Indeed, all hands had been under scrutiny during all these voyages; strengths and weaknesses among the men were quietly noted, and dispositions made that would capitalize on the one and contain the other until changes could be made. There were sixty-four Prince Edward Islanders in the *David's* crew; never again, swore the "Jimmy"*, would he sail with that many Islanders on board. Some of them were always on the rum; there was never a defaulter's list that did not name an Islander, and the Jimmy was finding it hard to come up with suitable punishments for them. As for Vernon, his transgressions ( at least, those that were detected) were minor. He once attempted to avoid Sunday Divisions by hiding in

---

* The Executive Officer, the second in command of a naval ship, responsible to the captain for the day-to-day running of the ship.

the canvas store, but was discovered and given seven days extra work as punishment. The seven days were served at sea; the extra work was not onerous, and no shore leave was lost, so Vernon felt that he came out of it well.

The months at sea were taking their toll on the ship; the time was coming when *Prince David* would need rest and refitting. That time arrived at the end of August 1941 when, after weathering a nasty summer storm in the Atlantic, the ship returned to Halifax. The crew were given thirty days leave so as to be out of the way, and the dockyard workers came on board to deal with the effects of wear and tear.

At home, Vernon's father had lately bought a newer car to replace the family Chevrolet. The replacement, a 1931 Plymouth sedan, had been so little driven and so lovingly cared for that it still had its original tires. On the second or third day of Vernon's leave, two of the old tires blew out, and with rubber in short supply they were not easily replaced. Vernon, who wanted above all to be mobile during his leave, would have been "grounded" had it not been for the generosity of his aunt and uncle who gave him full use of their car for the duration of his leave.

It was a wonderful leave. There was mother's cooking and baking to be enjoyed as never before. There was farm work if Vernon wanted to do it, or to be ignored if he didn't want to. There was a girl to court, and lots of his shipmates to party with. There was a ready audience of friends and family to hear his stories. The sea, and the perils of the sea, were set at a distance for a time. But only for a time. Leaves, like all good things, must end, and leaves seemed to end sooner than most things. By mid-October Vernon was back on board ship in Halifax, where preparations were under way for a long voyage and a change of coasts. Some English boy seamen came on board to make the trip to the west coast. Before left they had a taste of snow in Halifax, a novelty to them. That was soon a memory, however, as *Prince David* steamed south towards her Caribbean haunts. On this trip, though, island calls were strictly for oil and fresh provisions; the ship's immediate destination was the Panama Canal.

1. Fraser M. McKee, "Princes Three. Canada's Use of Armed Merchant Cruisers in World War II at V. RCN in Retrospect ed James A. Boutilier 120 - 121.

2. Joseph Shull, *The Far Distant Ships* (Ottawa: The Queen's Printer, 1952) 491.

3. Fritz-Otto Busch, *The Sinking of the Scharnhorst* (London: Futura Publications Ltd., 1975) 34

4. Martin Stephen, *The Fighting Admirals* (Annapolis Maryland: Naval Institute Press, 1991)

# 5. ANOTHER COAST, ANOTHER OCEAN:
## ESQUIMALT TO THE ALEUTIANS.

Land smells wafted across the water on hot humid air as *Prince David* slowed off Limon Bay to take on the Panama Canal pilot. With Vernon on the wheel, the pilot took the *David* past the breakwater into the bay and entered the seven-mile channel leading to the Gatun Locks. To port, had he had the time to look, Vernon would have seen the docks and waterfront of Cristobal on the bay's eastern shore. His full attention was on the wheel, however, and on the voice pipe from the bridge as the pilot brought *Prince David* slowly towards the open gates of the first of the three Gatun Locks. Silently, outside the lock entrance, the big ship stopped, her engines on "Stand By". Towing cables attached her to four squat, powerful locomotives, or "mules", which, two to a side, one forward and one aft, positioned her in the centre of the lock chamber. No longer required on the wheel, Vernon now had time to observe the operation of the Canal, and some details of its construction.

The lock gates were closed. The lock valves were opened. Over the next ten to twelve minutes inflowing water gently raised the ship to the level of the second lock. In an adjacent matching chamber an eastbound ship was being lowered to sea level. The mules were ready and waiting to pull the *David* through into the second chamber once the gates swung open. Again the gates were closed; again the water level rose, lifting the ship still higher above the level of the Atlantic ocean. A third time the ship was raised, but when the gates of the third chamber opened, the mules' cables were cast off, the pilot rang for "Slow Ahead, Both", and *Prince David* exited the lock under her own power into Gatun Lake, eighty-five feet above the sea level of the Atlantic Ocean.

Gatun Lake is a 163-square-mile impoundment created in the valley of the Chagres River. Before the canal was built, the Chagres flowed through its valley to empty into the Atlantic. When engineers built the Gatun Dam, the valley was flooded almost to the tops of the hills, which now are islands in this artificial lake. Water hyacinths have colonized the placid waters, their green leaves and purple flowers afloat on the surface, their subsurface vines a menace to propellers. Ships navigate a twenty-two mile long vegetation-free channel following the course of the drowned Chagres valley across Gatun Lake to the Gaillard cut, an eight mile trench, three hundred feet wide and forty-two or more feet deep. The canal builders excavated 211 million cubic yards of soil and rock to make the cut, but its sides are still so unstable that dredges work constantly clearing the channel of landslides. With skill and confidence born of years of experience, the pilot took *Prince David* across the lake and through the Gaillard cut to the Pedro Miguel Lock.

The Pedro Miguel Lock is the first of three steps which lower westbound ships down to the level of the Pacific ocean. The drop is thirty-one feet and, as at Gatun, mules positioned the ship in the lock chamber. Unlike Gatun, when the ship came out of the lock she had to steam a mile and a half across Miraflores

Lake to the next steps down, the two-chambered Miraflores Locks. Freed of these locks, the *David* steamed through an eight mile channel to pass Panama City and La Boca, dropped the pilot and entered Panama Bay. In a little more than eight hours she had been lifted eighty-five feet above sea level, had crossed some fifty miles of water, and been lowered again to sea level. In the process her voyage from Halifax to Esquimalt was made more than 6,000 miles shorter than by the only alternate route - around Cape Horn.

The first transit of the Panama Canal is an unforgettable experience for any sailor. Although attention to duty prevented him from taking in all the marvels of this wonder of the engineering world, impressions of that first passage remained vivid in Vernon's memory. He never forgot the ease with which his large ship was raised and lowered in the locks, the steep hillsides lining the Gaillard cut, and the dredges constantly at work keeping the channel clear. Though years later, as a merchant seaman, he made several more passages, this first one was a defining event in his career at sea.

In a few hours *Prince David* was clear of Panama Bay and steaming northwards in the Pacific. The first shore leave for Vernon and the ship's company was in San Diego, where the ship tied up at the foot of a wide street opening directly into the city. A Canadian warship was a novelty in this navy-wise city. Crowds turned out to see *Prince David*; entertainments were arranged for her officers and men; citizens opened their homes to the Canadian visitors. The two day stop-over, almost on the eve of Pearl Harbor, was a memorable one, and perhaps the last peace time gala in the city.

*Prince David's* arrival at Esquimalt was not auspicious: in a cross wind and blinding snow she bumped the gate ship, then lurched drunkenly towards the ammunition dock. Two hastily summoned tugs got lines on board and brought her under control but an inspection in drydock was deemed necessary. That meant deammunitioning, and deammunitioning meant extra work. No damage was found but while the ship was in the drydock a much needed ASDIC dome was fitted to her bottom.

The Burrard Drydock was at this time host to a famous lady of the seas, S.S. *Queen Elizabeth*. The "Q.E." was undergoing conversion to a troopship, and there was a lot of stripping, etc., to be done in her interior. A draft, which did not include Vernon, was sent from *Prince David* to help with the work. The hands returned full of awe for the great ship, in whose labyrinthine passages they often lost their way.

*Prince Robert* was in harbour, having just returned from escorting *Awatea* with the ill-fated "Force C", the Canadian army contingent, to Hong Kong. The *Robert* had passed through Honolulu just three days before the Japanese attack on December 7, 1941, totally unaware of the imminence of that strike. It was the first time since their commissioning that these two Princes had met.

That December in Esquimalt was wet and cool. There did not seem to be much to do and the *David* languished in the dockyard. No-one had any clear idea of whether the Japanese posed a threat; if they did, it looked like the two Princes were the counter but no plan of action had yet been formed.

For Vernon, this quiet time was an opportunity to look up some relatives. Both his father and his mother had cousins who had "gone west" just before or after the Great War and when he had shore leave Vernon set out to find them. George Drake, his father's first cousin, who grew up on the next farm to Vernon's home, operated a dairy in New Westminster;  Vernon found him and was most hospitably received. Wilbur MacLaren, his mother's second cousin, was a fire-fighter in Vancouver; Vernon and shipmate Henry Davy visited Wilbur and his family in their neat home on 13th Avenue over the Christmas holiday period. It was only Vernon's second Christmas away from home, and his first away from the Maritimes; he remembers it as having more rain than snow.

The winter passed slowly, with patrols up and down the coast. *Prince David's* third skipper, Captain V. S. Godfrey RCN, was an avid fisherman to whom these salmon-rich waters were irresistible. Vernon recalls more than one occasion when he was called as coxswain of the fast motor boat (the skimming dish, it was called) to take his captain fishing. Vernon, too, enjoyed fishing, and would have gladly wet a line, but angling privileges did not apply to ratings when the captain went fishing. Whether the captain's casts ever boated a sockeye for the wardroom table is unrecorded, but there was a sure way of obtaining a fish dinner for the crew: a depth charge dropped in the right spot would bring a bonanza of stunned fish to the surface. They had only to be gathered in for will-ing cook's helpers to prepare salmon steaks.

In April, *Prince David* began a short refit. Leave was granted and Vernon made his first trans-Canada train trip. The Navy provided a ticket but on the over-crowded trains it was no guarantee of a seat. No sleeping berth was provided, and even if one were available, an Able Seaman could not afford it. But sailors have a special ingenuity for finding a place "to get their heads down", and careful frat-ernizing with the conductor assured Vernon and a friend a place in the baggage car. It was rough, and kitbags made a lumpy bed, but it was possible to sleep. Never a gambler, Vernon did not join any of the many non-stop poker games by which many fellow-travellers whiled away their nights and days.

By day the boys had the spectacle of Canada to marvel at: the towering Rockies; the break in the trip at Jasper; the vast breadth of the prairies; the iso-lation of the Canadian Shield; and the industrial bustle of the east, now geared to wartime production. It all could have been wonderful except for one thing - time. Vernon had three weeks leave, and two of those weeks were used in coming and going. He had six precious days at home.

He arrived unannounced. Any letter he would have written to tell his par-ents of his coming would, at the best, have travelled on the same train as he did, and allowing for sorting time, might reach its destination a day after his arrival. A telegram was not really an option; telegrams already had an ominous portent, and were to be avoided except in special emergencies. So, late one night in April, Vernon was joyously received in the warm farm kitchen in Meadow Bank. As always, the days of furlough flew by, and pangs of parting followed swiftly on the joys of homecoming.

*Prince Henry*, which had been operating in the Caribbean during the winter, arrived in Esquimalt in early May, shortly after Vernon's return from leave, thus completing the reunion of the Princes Three. Together they would face the Japanese, should they dare to come, but first they would get some modernization. ASDIC had now been fitted in all three; plastic armour was added to the open bridges; and several 20-mm Oerlikon cannons were mounted to enhance anti-air-craft defences. Perhaps as important as these modest improvements was a listing of specific duties:

*1. guard the focal points for shipping in the northeast Pacific, par-ticularly off British Columbia;*
*2. patrol sheltered waters where enemy vessels might hide along the coast;*
*3. reassure the public by their presence;*
*4. satisfy American demands for a Canadian naval force in the area;*
*5. make credible threats designed to keep the enemy away.[1]*

How many of these objectives were really within the capabilities of the Princes is questionable, but they pitched into their assignments with vigour. The fact that during their "watch" the only enemy activity on the west coast of Canada was the ineffectual shelling of the Estevan lighthouse might be taken as a measure of their effectiveness, but the reality was that Japanese Imperial Forces never really got around to that part of the world.

There was time that summer of 1942 to excuse the *Prince David* from duty in the real war in favour of a role in a make-believe conflict. Hollywood was turning out a steady run of war-theme movies designed as morale boosters as much as money makers. "Commandos Strike At Dawn", starring Paul Muni and Lillian Gish, was a fair example of the genre. It was the story of a pacifist Norwegian who, disgusted with the brutality of the Nazi invaders of his country, escapes to England and offers to lead a Commando raid on a Luftwaffe airfield being constructed near his home village in Norway. The west coast of British Columbia was sufficiently like Norwegian topography for Hollywood's purpos-es; all that was needed was a ship to act as the transport for the commando force.

Enter *Prince David* and her crew. The film makers would embark daily in *Prince David* to film sequences of shipboard life and the landing of the strike force. It was all great fun for the ship's company. First, there was the presence of the stars; bringing them off in the mornings and returning them to shore in the evenings were much sought after duties. Then there were the technical mixups, as for example having a seaman sound with leadline* and call back to the bridge depths in which the ship would have been hard aground; or the Officer of the Watch ordering a change of course to starboard and having the ship's head turn to port. During "takes" all crew were supposed to be out of sight of the camera and quiet. More than one scene was ruined by a careless matelot wandering onto the set or by a loud burst of naval profanity from the sidelines.

---

* In a ship, "feeling its way" in shallow waters of unknown depth, one or more seamen were sta-tioned forward with a lead-weighted line which was dropped in the water to ascertain the depth in fathoms, which information was called back to the bridge.

Notwithstanding their unsolicited participation in movie making, the crew had an opportunity to make cameo appearances in the film. Vernon's big five seconds came as Paul Muni's character was about to enter the landing craft which would take him and the troops ashore. For some reason never clear from the movie's plot, he removed his coat before going over the side; Vernon was the sailor standing by who dutifully took the coat. Back home, we had been apprised by Vernon's letters of his movie career, and when "Commandos Strike At Dawn" came to Charlottetown, family and friends were among the first at the theatre. Unfortunately, Vernon's appearance on the screen was so brief that they were never certain that they had seen him.

There was, as it turned out, a certain irony in *Prince David's* playacting: in just a few months she would undergo renovation for a new career very similar to her "let's pretend" role in the movie. When her renovation was completed she would be an Infantry Landing Ship.

That was still in the future. In June, Japanese Vice -Admiral Moshira Hosogaya led the carriers *Ryujo* and *Junyo*, with three 8-inch cruisers and three light cruisers, to the Aleutian Islands. On June 3 and 4 his planes bombed Dutch Harbor, and on June 7 he landed amphibious forces on two of the outermost islands of the Aleutian chain, Attu and Kiska. Twelve hundred troops went ashore on Attu and 1250 on Kiska. There was no opposition, as neither of the islands had occupants. An attack on Adak was called off.

The U.S. Navy had two 8-inch and three 6-inch cruisers based in Dutch Harbour, but they were patrolling four hundred miles south of Kodiak. Because of prevailing bad visibility, the two small fleets never found each other.

The purpose of this bloodless invasion was partly to anchor a Japanese line of defense roughly 2,000 miles east of the Homeland, from Kiska through Midway to New Guinea. Successful establishment of the perimeter required the capture of Midway Island, and the Aleutian adventure was partly a diversionary tactic calculated to draw some American strength away from that island. Unfortunately for the Japanese the Battle of Midway was their first major naval setback. Admiral Yamamato lost four aircraft carriers in the battle, and the tide of the Pacific war turned irrevocably in favour of the Americans. The small Japanese Task Force in the Aleutions was not reinforced and was eventually withdrawn.

The American response to the Japanese presence was to send troops and supplies to Kodiak whence an expedition to recover Attu and Kiska would be mounted. Orders came to Esquimalt for the RCN to assist the Americans in their Aleutian campaign, and on August 20, 1942 the three Princes, preceded by the corvettes *Dawson* and *Vancouver*, steamed north to Dutch Harbor. Ahead were two months of convoy work along the Aleutian chain in some of the world's worst waters. If it was not blowing, it was foggy. When it was blowing, it could be a howling, icy gale out of Bering Strait or it could be the "williwaws" - sudden, clawing Alaskan winds, pregnant with precipitation. Add to these the hazards of uncharted shoals, and erratic currents flowing only they knew where, and who needed contact with the enemy? The enemy was there, for a time at least, but the Canadian ships did not meet him before their departure south in mid-November.

Patrolling the British Columbia coast was resumed, but reality was finally setting in at Naval Headquarters, where even ardent supporters (if there were any such) of the Princes Three were forced to admit that these ships could neither protect convoys nor themselves from a determined attack by enemy warships. If investments in them to date were not to be lost, some new role for them had to be found. In early 1943, strategic planning for future combined operations in Europe had identified the need for large vessels like the Princes to carry troops. It was decided that *Prince David* and *Prince Henry* would be converted to Landing Ships Infantry(Medium). To this end the *Henry* went into the Burrard Drydock on April 30, 1943, and the *David* the next day.

HMCS *Prince Robert* had been taken out of service at the beginning of 1943 for conversion to an auxiliary anti-aircraft cruiser. Armed with modern weaponry - 10 HA/LA 4-inch in twin mounts, 8 pom-poms and 12 Oerlikons - she came out of her refit as one of the most powerful A.A. ships for her size afloat. By October of 1943 she was providing vital A.A. protection to convoys between England and Naples. On her very first trip, she drove off two Heinkels carrying Fritz-X radio-controlled bombs, of which more will be written later.

*Prince David* was recommissioned on December 20, 1943, and *Prince Henry* on January 6, 1944. They left Esquimalt for the Atlantic in mid-January, still with many deficiencies that would have to be corrected later in the U.K.. The *David* carried 437 American soldiers from New York to Scotland, and the *Henry* returned 250 British school children evacuated from Britain to Bermuda during the blitz of 1940. The ships spent several weeks in the John Browns Clydebank yards to complete their fitting out before going south to the Isle of Wight for sea training.

In the two and one quarter years of their first commissions, the Princes Three and the men who served in them, with the possible exception of *Prince Robert,* had had an uneventful war. *Prince David*, especially, had been  incredibly lucky in that, having been "in harm's way", no harm had come to her. The size of the Princes far exceeded their offensive and defensive powers, and in any action with the surface raiders the enemy sent to sea, they would have fared disastrously. Some post-war Naval historians have questioned the wisdom of ever having converted them to Armed Merchant Cruisers, and credit their lives in that role to grandiose ideas of a big ship navy held by Rear-Admiral Percy Nelles. Critics argue that, given the naval manpower crisis of 1940 and the mounting successes of the U-boat campaign in the Atlantic, the 1300 officers and men crewing the Princes would have been better employed manning eight more four-stacker destroyers or fifteen more corvettes.[2] Certainly, Canada's sea war was in the Atlantic, and Canada's principal sea warriors were her almost 200 corvettes and frigates and their ship's companies, operating with our 26 destroyers. If, through no fault of their own, the Prince ships and their complements had contributed little to the efforts at sea up to mid-war, their time, and their opportunities, were not far ahead.

When *Prince David* went for conversion, most of her crew was dispersed. Vernon and a shipmate, Al Hunt, applied for, and were accepted to a Leading Seaman's course at HMCS *Naden*, the training barracks at Esquimalt. It was a gruelling, "at the double" six to eight-week course, during which the trainees never left the barracks. The class was refreshed in visual signalling skills: Morse code, semaphore and international code. They learned anchor and cable routines, advanced gunnery skills and parade ground command. They even had three days at sea in a Bangor minesweeper, a real change for Vernon and Al Hunt. It was Vernon's first taste of life ashore since completion of his basic training, and his first "school work" in a long time, and he wondered how he would do in his passing out exam. He need not have worried; he fared well in his finals, and on June 17, 1943, he was rated Leading Seaman and LR III.

The two Maritimers wanted to get back east and approached the Manning Officer with their requests for transfer. Hunt was first in line. "Reason for this request?", asked the officer. "I want to see some action, Sir, and there's none on this coast", replied Hunt. "So it's action you want, is it", said the officer; then turning to Vernon he said, "And I suppose your excuse is the same as Hunt's?". "Yes, sir!', replied Vernon, who was not at all sure he was being truthful. "Granted", said the officer, and four days later the two friends were drafted to *Stadacona*.

Over the summer, the two new "killicks", as Leading Seamen were familiarly known, did killick's work in Halifax: drilling new entries; supervising work parties; mounting guards; and doing shore patrols (disciplinary parties on the streets). It was not Vernon's favourite form of Navy life, but he need not have worried. Having professed a craving for action, he would soon be leaving "Stad" for something much more to his liking.

1. Fraser M. McKee, "Princes Three. Canada's Use of Armed Merchant Cruisers in World War II. in RCN in Retrospect, ed James A. Boutilier. 124 - 125.

2. Tony German, The Sea Is At Our Gates (Toronto: McCelland and Stewart, 1990) 96.

a).

a). *HMCS Prince David entering Willemstad, Curacao, Dutch West Indies.*

b).

b). *Prince David drydocked in Bermuda for inspection of damage after grounding while entering Hamilton harbour.*

a).

b).

*HMCS Prince David*
a). *Looking aft from the bow: "A" gun (lower) and "B" gun. The shield extending forward over "A" gun protected its gun's crew from the muzzle blast and flash of "B" gun. The scuttles ("portholes") behind "B" gun are in the wheelhouse, which is topped by the bridge. Twin Lewis guns flank the wheelhouse. The matting above and below the wheelhouse was to protect against shell splinters. Note the crowsnest on the foremast, above the bridge.*
b). *Gun shield and breach of "A" gun. The 6-inch projectiles (shells) are in cradles around the gun; they were the "ready-use" ammunition to supply the gun until more could be brought up from the shell room below decks.*

*Rough weather. I.*
*a). <u>Prince David</u> on convoy escort, lifeboats slung outboard for hasty launching if necessary. A storm is brewing; the rising wind is starting to whip the crests off the waves.*

*b). A wave rising steeply on the lee side.*

*Rough weather. II.*
*a). A towering wave on the weather side. In the roaring wind and welter of water, the watch is trying to secure the boat to its griping spar to prevent it being smashed and/or carried away.*

*b). Coming over white. A wall of spray, bridge-high, comes over <u>Prince Davids</u> bow and drenches the fo'c's'le on its way aft.*

*Vernon with new friends at the American naval base, Trinidad.*

*Liberty Boat*
*Ordinary Seamen Drake and Llewellyn in their tropical whites, ready for shore leave in San Fernando, Trinidad.*

*Touring Trinidad in a rented car.*

a).

b).

*Shipboard life. I.*
*a). Vernon working with a hawser on <u>Prince David's</u> quarterdeck. He should not have been smoking!*
*b). Caulking seams on the deck of the bridge. The dark round object on the right is part of the binnacle housing the magnetic compass; it helped insulate the compass magnets from the effect of surrounding steel. Another illicit smoker!*

Shipboard life. II.

a). Dhobey day. Doing one's washing on deck. The large pipe in the background is the ship's degaussing gear.

b). Sailors are chronically short of sleep, and when it is hot below it is nice to "flake out" in a shady spot on deck. The shade which these two ratings chose has moved away while they slept.

*In the Panama Canal. Pictures by Vernon during a postwar transit of the Canal, when he was a merchant seaman.*
*a). Approaching a lock chamber as the lock gates open.*
*b). In the lock, which is filling and lifting the ship.*

a).

*a). Watch on deck, dressed for wet weather. West Coat, 1942.*
*b). Bundled up against the "williwaws". Alaska, 1942.*
*c). Able Seaman and Old Salt.*
*A/B Vernon Drake, dressed for going ashore, Halifax, September 1941.*

a).

b).

c).

*a). Vernon in working dress, <u>Prince David's</u> quarterdeck, Esquimalt.*
*b). Actors Lillian Gish and Paul Muni, with one of <u>Prince David's</u> officers, during a break in filming <u>Commandos Strike At Dawn.</u>*
*c). Vernon and friends enjoy a break from the train on their way home on leave.*

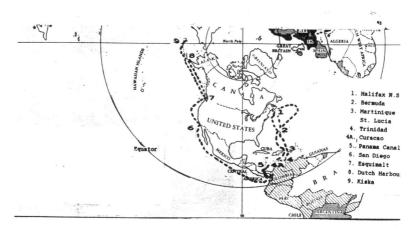

a).

1. Halifax N.S
2. Bermuda
3. Martinique
   St. Lucia
4. Trinidad
4A. Curacao
5. Panama Canal
6. San Diego
7. Esquimalt
8. Dutch Harbour
9. Kiska

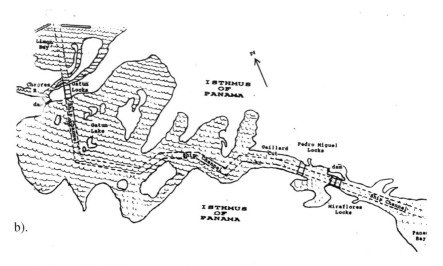

b).

*a). Cruise of HMCS Prince David as Armed Merchant Cruiser,*
*December 28, 1940 - April 30, 1943.*
*b). The Panama Canal. (Diagramatic and not to scale.)*

# 6. CRUISERS: VERY SPECIAL SHIPS.

There were cruisers in the Royal Navy when it was a navy under sail; certain large frigates were at times deployed to operate independently against raiders of merchant ships.[1] During the transition from sail to steam, and from wooden hulls to steel, the cruiser concept remained valid.

British cruisers, as they evolved during the first half of the twentieth century, were arguably the most versatile warships in commission. They were fast and manoeuverable; they had long cruising ranges; they were well armoured and well armed. Their main armament was 9 or 12 six-inch or larger guns, with a secondary armament of four-inch guns; pom-poms (2-pd, in quads), Oerlikons (20mm quick firing cannom); and torpedo tubes. For a time, they even carried one or two aircraft (amphibious Walruses). Thus equipped, they could operate independently to protect or to harass trade. They were equally useful in fleet work, screening battleships and aircraft carriers in their task forces, as well as bringing a superior enemy to bay and containing him until appropriate force could effect his destruction. They had the weight of shell to be dangerous adversaries of enemy surface warships as well as being effective in bombarding land targets. At the Battle of the River Plate, three cruisers, *Ajax, Exeter* and *Achilles*, hounded *Graf Spee* to her doom; cruisers assisted in the sinking of *Bismarck* and of *Scharnhorst*. Cruisers escorted convoys in the Mediterranean, and on the Murmansk run. In the Bay of Biscay the cruisers HMS *Glasgow* and *Enterprise* engaged a vastly superior force of eleven German destroyers, sinking three of them and driving the remainder to the safety of port. (More detail on that action later.) In amphibious landing operations, first in the Mediterranean, later off Normandy, and in the days after D-Day, cruisers served as sea-based artillery whose guns gave close support to the invasion forces advancing through the first few miles behind the beaches.

Because of their versatility and of the great variety of tasks they were called upon to perform, these ships took more than their fair share of lumps during the war. Of the sixty-four Royal Navy cruisers in commission at the beginning of World War II, thirty-two were sunk or scrapped in the conflict. These losses were all made good through wartime replacements, and sixty-five cruisers were in service at war's end, with five more under construction.[2]

The RCN began in 1910 with two cruisers: HMCS *Niobe*, an obsolecent large cruiser based in Halifax from October 21, 1910; and HMCS *Rainbow*, a smaller vessel, based in Esquimalt from November of the same year[3]. When war came in 1914, crews were somehow cobbled together for them, but neither ship was an effective man-o'-war. *Rainbow* made a brave sortie or two down the west coast, but *Niobe* never ventured far from port. She was in commission for only a year or so of the war before being paid off as unfit for hostilities, and *Rainbow* went the same way in 1917. (Two of *Niobe's* 1895-vintage 6-inch guns were part of the World War II defenses of St. John harbour, and her name sailed on as an RCN shore establishment, HMCS *Niobe*, at Plymouth, England, until June 30,

1941, and at Greenock, Scotland, from December 15, 1941 until 1945) From 1920 until she was sold in 1922, another cruiser, the *Aurora*, was an HMC Ship. From then on, the Canadian Government introduced a series of budget cuts which threatened the very continued existence of a Canadian navy. No Chief of Naval Staff dared dream of cruiser-size ships in his navy until 1940 when the urgency of a new war brought a fresh realism to naval budgeting. The conversion of the Princes Three to Armed Merchant Cruisers gave the RCN three "big ships", but even then the developing Battle of the Atlantic imposed a strategic imperative that demanded first emphasis on the building, crewing and deployment of small escort ships - the corvettes ("Canada's Flowers") and frigates which came to be the hallmark of the Royal Canadian Navy in the Second World War. Only when ascendance over Admiral Doenitz's U-boats had been achieved, and the trans-Atlantic convoy routes made safe for commerce, would it be timely to think of adding to the fleet ships larger than destroyers.

That time came in August, 1943, at the Quebec Conference. In preparation for the conference, the general requirements for Canadian participation in the naval war against Japan and a vision of a post-war Canadian navy were set out. Although, at this time, Allied strategy against Japan, and Canada's place within such a strategy, had not been fully worked out, the Department of Planning for the Chief of Naval Staff felt that to fulfil its future commitments the RCN would require cruisers, aircraft carriers and fleet destroyers.

On August 11, 1943, (the opening day of the Quebec Conference) the Chief of Naval Staff put it to the First Lord of the Admiralty that he did not want to see the RCN emerge from the war as a navy of small ships only, and that he saw Canada's post-war navy comprising five cruisers, two light fleet carriers and three destroyer flotillas, with a number of smaller vessels.

Canadians entered the ensuing discussions from a perspective of building a new kind of naval force. The Admiralty had a different perspective. Its reaction was influenced, in part at least, by a developing manpower crisis in the U.K. which would prevent the manning of HM ships already under construction. It was eventually agreed that Canada would acquire from Britain, and man with Canadian personnel, at least one cruiser - possibly two - and two fleet destroyers.

The Canadian navy had lots of experience with destroyers. Adding two more to the fleet presented few logistical problems. Nor was the manning and maintaining of cruisers seen as a serious problem for the RCN; after all, the ships were really just "a step up" from Tribal Class destroyers, with which the navy was already familiar. Aircraft carriers were another matter, however, involving as they would the creation of a Fleet Air Arm. A decision on the carriers was deferred.

As to the correct protocol for transferring the ships, it was decided to have Prime Minister Churchill make a request, on behalf of the First Sea Lord, to Prime Minister MacKenzie King to assist the Admiralty with its manpower shortage by providing crews for two cruisers and two destroyers. On September 8, 1943, the Cabinet War Committee essentially acceded to this request, provided that no additional manpower would be required by the Navy. In November, 1943, it was decided to scale back production of Canadian frigates and corvettes, and to draft the personnel so freed up to man the RN ships being transferred to the RCN.

In January, 1944, it was proposed that two RCN task forces, each comprising two cruisers, one carrier, and eight or nine destroyers, be sent to the Pacific. This proposal grew from an earlier memo which envisaged a post-war fleet of four cruisers, two light fleet carriers, sixteen fleet destroyers, six frigates and a number of minesweepers.

Serious planning for Canada's naval presence in the Pacific began in May, 1944 at a Commonwealth Conference in London. The Admiralty at first suggested a fleet of two cruisers, two escort carriers, two destroyers and numerous smaller units. In subsequent development of the proposal the number and types of ship were changed a little, and a total commitment of 22,000 men was made. Then, on October 11, 1944, the Cabinet War Committee ruled that the total manpower commitment should be slightly more than 13,400, a little more than half of what Naval Staff had planned for. This manpower restriction set the final pattern for the RCN's force against the Japanese. Two cruisers and two carriers.would go to the Pacific, with *Prince Robert* as an Auxiliary A.A. ship, along with ten destroyers and about forty frigates and corvettes.

Meanwhile, the war was raging on, and the exchange of ships could not be delayed until every detail of planning for the Pacific campaign had been worked out. The destroyers were the first units to be transferred. In February, 1944 the V-Class destroyers HMS *Valentine* and *Vixen* were recommissioned as HMCS *Algonquin* and *Sioux*, respectively. The cruisers destined for transfer were still under construction. They were to be HMS *Minotaur* and *Superb*, 8,800 ton vessels mounting nine 6-inch guns, ten 4-inch guns and two banks of 21" torpedo tubes. They were in most respects similar to *Fiji*-class cruisers, except that they were to have an entirely new fire control system for their guns - the most modern system afloat. But technical problems with this new system, plus shortages of labour and materials, had put the completion dates of these ships, especially of *Superb*, away behind schedule. Accordingly, it was decided to substitute HMS *Uganda*, a modified *Fiji*-class ship, for *Superb*, and to accept *Minotaur* when she was completed.

In November, 1943, *Uganda* had gone to the dockyard in Charleston, North Carolina, for extensive repair and refit after sustaining heavy damage from a German bomb. She would be recommissioned HMCS *Uganda* on Trafalgar Day, 1944. HMS *Minotaur* would join the RCN as HMCS *Ontario* in April, 1945, one month before VE Day. With the Admiralty's gift of these two new powerful warships, Canada would truly have "big ships" in her navy.

Very soon after initial planning for the expansion of Canada's fleet started, the first moves were made toward manning the ships to come. Some Canadian officers, for one reason or another, had already served in HM ships, including cruisers, and would be a valuable resource. There was an urgent need for seaman gunners with some experience on 6-inch; they could be found most readily among crews of the Prince ships. This was probably why Vernon, now a Leading Seaman and an LR/III, was selected as one among some eighty ratings from the Volunteer Reserve for cruiser training with the Royal Navy. The RN ships initially assigned to training the Canadians were HMS *Belfast, Bermuda, Glasgow, Jamaica. Nigeria,* and *Sheffield.*

Vernon was enjoying some autumn leave at home when he was recalled to Halifax to await transport to the UK. The Navy decided to send the entire draft of cruiser trainees by troopship. They were embarked as passengers in S.S. *Mauritania* at Halifax late in October 1943.

It was not a pleasant voyage. Vastly outnumbered by the thousands of army and hundreds of Air Force troops on board, the Navy lads fared badly in the interminable lineups for the two meals served daily, and meals were missed. Very quickly, the sailors learned to forage for themselves for sustenance. This was the first ocean voyage for most of the passengers, and the Atlantic in late October was not the gentlest water. Many of the passengers were seasick, making 'tween-decks an unwholesome place to be. Vernon and his mates were berthed four decks down. Just to get topside for fresh air was a struggle; any hope of reaching the bridge was but a dream. At night all troops were confined below decks. By order, Mae West lifejackets were worn at all times.

The lifejackets, fortunately, were never needed. *Mauritania* was a fast ship, relying on her speed as her defense against U-boats. Even steering a zigzag course, she made the crossing to Liverpool in a few days. After disembarkation, the sailors went north by train to HMCS *Niobe*, the RCN manning and pay establishment at Greenock on the River Clyde. The smaller trains and the coaches with passenger compartments and no aisles were something new to the lads from Canada, but the overcrowding was familiar from rail travel back home.

It was raining when the little band of Canadians reached *Niobe* on November 2, 1943. Their accommodation was a series of large bell tents, and the inexperienced campers were warned not, on any account, to touch the inner surface of the canvas. A psychologist might have issued instructions to the contrary, knowing that to prohibit something is the surest way to get young persons to do it. Sure enough, in many a tent many a finger was rubbed against the protective canvas, and sure enough, a leak developed wherever contact had been made. Vernon spent only two nights under canvas. By virtue of his rating as Leading Seaman he was entitled to a bunk in a more or less heated barrack block. As he recalls, he never had to sling his hammock during his entire stay at Greenock.

Life at *Niobe* was largely a matter of killing time. Normal naval routine, including Divisions, was suspended for the personnel awaiting drafts. Rumours were rife about the ships to which the lads might be sent. On what basis no-one ever knew or cared to know, this ship was reputed to be "happy", that ship was feared as "unlucky" and so on. Vernon kept his ear open to these rumours, and when the reports were unfavourable (as they most often were) he would go to the base dentist for tooth repairs, which would effectively stop his draft. Every day, however, some of the group of Canadians would be claimed. Some went to HMS *Liverpool*, whose bows were blown off by a torpedo and ignition of airplane fuel on her next trip. Some, including Joe LeClair, went to HMS *Sheffield*, then on the Murmansk convoy run. Jack Thomson went to HMS *Jamaica*. Vernon almost got sent to HMS *Nigeria* but, as he says, he had one bad tooth left, and it saved him one more time. When his name appeared on a draft to HMS *Glasgow*, his teeth had all been repaired, the dentist was beginning to suspect malingering, and Vernon had to go. Perhaps there had been something to the rumours going around *Niobe*; perhaps it was just blind good luck, but now that his number was up he went, with a dozen others, to a fine fighting ship in which he would join a well-trained professional crew under a fine captain and excellent officers.

They went by night train from Glasgow, his new ship's namesake city, to London and on to Portsmouth for a brief stay until proceeding to Plymouth where HMS *Glasgow* was berthed. For Vernon, new Navy experiences and some real war were ahead.

1. *HMS Belfast.* (London: Imperial War Museum, 1999.) 32.

2. Geoffrey Bennett, *Naval Battles of World War II.* (London: B.T.Botsford, 1975.) 41.

3. Daniel Hannington, "75 Years of Service" in *Canada's Navy. A Wings Commemorative Issue.* (Calgary: Corvus Publishing Group, 1985) 21.

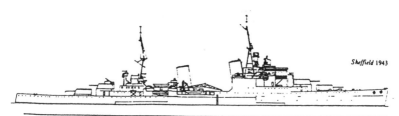

*Sheffield* 1943

---

## SOUTHAMPTON class     **HMS** *Glasgow*

| | |
|---|---|
| **Displacement:** | 9100t standard; 11,350t (later 12,190t) deep load |
| **Dimensions:** | 558ft pp, 591ft 6in oa × 61ft 8in × 20ft 4in (later 21ft 6in) mean deep load<br>*170.07, 180.28 × 18.79 × 6.20 (6.55)m* |
| **Machinery:** | 4-shaft Parsons geared turbines, 4 Admiralty 3-drum boilers, 75,000shp = 32kts. Oil 1925–2070t |
| **Armour:** | Box protection to ammunition spaces 4½in–1in, belt 4½in, bulkheads 2½in, turrets 1in, trunks and ring bulkheads 2in–1in |
| **Armament:** | 12–6in/50 Mk XXIII (4×3), 8–4in/45 QF Mk XVI HA (4×2), 4–3pdr saluting, 8–2pdr pompom (2×4), 6–21in TT aw (2×3), 3 aircraft |
| **Complement:** | 748 |

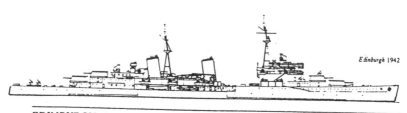

*Edinburgh* 1942

---

## EDINBURGH class     **HMS** *Belfast*

| | |
|---|---|
| **Displacement:** | 10,550t standard; 13,175t (*Belfast* later 14,900t) deep load |
| **Dimensions:** | 579ft pp, 613ft 6in oa × 63ft 4in (*Belfast* later 66ft 4in) × 21ft 3in (*Belfast* later 23ft 2in) mean deep load<br>*176.47, 186.99 × 19.30 (20.22) × 6.48 (7.06)m* |
| **Machinery:** | 4-shaft Parsons geared turbines, 4 Admiralty 3-drum boilers, 80,000shp = 32.5kts. Oil 2250t (later 1990t) |
| **Armour:** | Belt 4½in, bulkheads 2½in, turrets 4in–2in, ring bulkheads 2in–1in |
| **Armament:** | 12–6in/50 Mk XXIII (4×3), 12–4in/45 QF Mk XVI HA (6×2), 4–3pdr saluting, 16–2pdr pompom (2×8), 6–21in TT aw (2×3), 3 aircraft |
| **Complement:** | 850 |

*Above and following page:*

*Some classes of cruisers in Royal Navy or Royal Canadian Navy service during or immediately after World War Two. Not every class of cruiser mentioned in this narrative is included: for example, HMS* Enterprise *was an Emerald Class light cruiser, laid down June 28, 1918.*

*These pages adapted from material supplied by Information Room, Naval Historical Branch, Imperial War Museum.*

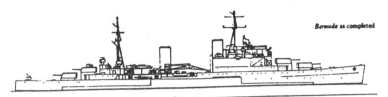

*Bermuda* as completed

## FIJI class    ~~HMS/HMCS~~ *Uganda*

| | |
|---|---|
| **Displacement:** | 8530t standard; 10,450t (later 10,830–11,090t) deep load |
| **Dimensions:** | 538ft pp, 555ft 6in oa × 62ft × 19ft 10in (later 20ft 4in–20ft 9in) mean deep load<br>*163.98, 169.31 × 18.90 × 6.04 (6.20–6.32)m* |
| **Machinery:** | 4-shaft Parsons geared turbines, 4 Admiralty 3-drum boilers, 72,500shp = 31.5kts. Oil 1613–1700t |
| **Armour:** | Belt 3¼in–3½in, bulkheads 2in–1½in, turrets 2in–1in, ring bulkheads 1in max |
| **Armament:** | 12–6in/50 Mk XXIII (4×3) (*Ceylon, Newfoundland, Uganda* 9–6in/50 Mk XXIII (3×3)) 8–4in/45 QF<br>Mk XVI HA (4×2), 8–2pdr pompom (2×4) (*Ceylon, Newfoundland, Uganda* 12–2pdr pompom (3×4)),<br>6–21in TT aw (2×3), 2 aircraft |
| **Complement:** | 730; 920 war |

*Black Prince* 1943

## BELLONA class    HMS *Black Prince*

| | |
|---|---|
| **Displacement:** | 5950t standard; 7350–7410t deep load |
| **Dimensions:** | 485ft pp, 512ft oa × 50ft 6in × 17ft 9in–17ft 11in mean deep load<br>*147.82, 156.05 × 15.39 × 5.41–5.46m* |
| **Machinery:** | 4-shaft Parsons geared turbines, 4 Admiralty 3-drum boilers, 62,000shp = 32kts. Oil 1042–1100t |
| **Armour:** | Side 3in, bulkheads 1in |

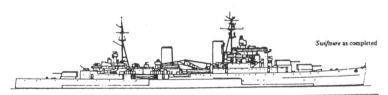

*Swiftsure* as completed

## SWIFTSURE class    HMCS *Ontario*

| | |
|---|---|
| **Displacement:** | 8800t standard; 11,130t (*Swiftsure* later 11,240t, *Ontario* 11,480t) deep load |
| **Dimensions:** | 538ft pp, 555ft 6in oa × 63ft × 20ft 8in (later 20ft 10in–21ft 2in) mean deep load<br>*163.98, 169.31 × 19.20 × 6.30 (6.35–6.45)m* |
| **Machinery:** | 4-shaft Parsons geared turbines, 4 Admiralty 3-drum boilers, 72,500shp = 31.5kts. Oil 1850t |
| **Armour:** | Belt 3¼in–3½in, bulkheads 2in–1½in, turrets 2in–1in, ring bulkheads 1in max |
| **Armament:** | 9–6in/50 Mk XXIII (3×3), 10–4in/45 QF Mk XVI HA (5×2), 16–2pdr pompom (4×4), 6–21in TT aw<br>(2×3) |
| **Complement:** | 855; 960 war |

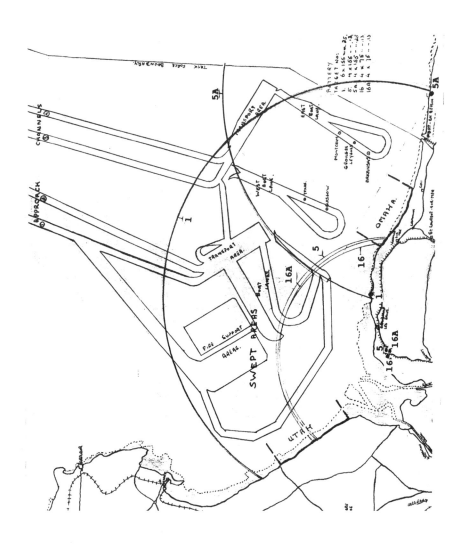

*A page from Midshipman Balfour's personal log, showing the Normandy coast at "Omaha" and "Utah" beaches, morning of June 6, 1944. Sites of the defending batteries, their strength and their arcs of fire seaward are shown; mineswept channels, anchorages and assembly areas for the invasion forces are plotted, as are the initial positions of Task Force 124.*

## 7. HMS GLASGOW: A FIGHTING SHIP.

HMS *Glasgow* was a *Southampton*-class cruiser, a larger type of ship designed to match more closely the pattern of building in other between-the-wars navies. The namesake of the class. HMS *Southampton*, and her sister, HMS *Newcastle*, were laid down in 1934. The remainder of the class, HM Ships *Sheffield*, *Glasgow* and *Birmingham*, were laid down in 1935. All were launched in 1936 and commissioned in 1937. All survived the war except *Southampton*; hit by two or three 550-lb bombs which set off uncontrollable fires in the superstructure and the forward boiler room, she had to be abandoned. She sank January 11, 1941, torpedoed by HMS *Gloucester* and HMS *Orion*.

HMS *Glasgow* was laid down at Scott's Shipbuilding and Engineering Co. Ltd, Greenock on April 16, 1935.[1] She was launched on June 20, 1936 by Mrs. Stanley Baldwin, the wife of the British Prime Minister, becoming the fourth Royal Navy ship to bear the name. She was commissioned September 8th, 1937, a day before the official date of completion. Even so, she was not "completed", since she did not receive her HA gunnery control until December.

*Glasgow* was 591feet 6inches long, with a beam of 61feet 8 inches. Her draught was 20feet 3inches forward, and 20feet 10inches aft. Her displacement was 9,100 tons. Four Admiralty 3-drum boilers raised steam to drive four Parsons shaft geared turbines capable of 75,000 shaft horsepower. At full power, her speed was thirty-two knots. In her bunkers she had capacity for 2,070 tons of fuel oil, allowing her a range of 10,400 miles at twelve knots; at full speed she would consume all her fuel over the course of 2,800 miles.

*Glasgow's* protective armour included four-and-one-half-inch belt;* box protection to similar thickness for the ammunition spaces; two-and-one-half-inch bulkheads; one inch on the turrets; and two inches on the ring bulkheads supporting the turrets. The armament comprised twelve 6-inch Mk XXIII guns in four triple turrets; eight 4-inch Quick Firing Mk XVI High Angle guns in four double mounts; four 3-pounders; eight 2-pounder pom-poms in two quadruple mounts; six 21-inch torpedo tubes; and two Walrus aircraft. Her commissioning complement was forty-seven officers and 692 ratings.

Historically, HM Ships christened *Glasgow* amassed a list of battle honours beginning with Lagos in 1759. The ship that Vernon joined at Portsmouth had already added three World War II actions to that list: Norway 1940; Arctic 1943; and, perhaps the most glorious of all, Biscay 1943. This last action was so recent that its aftermath was clearly visible to the newcomers in blistered paint on the guns, in pock marks from shell fragments and in a casualty list. Although the Canadian boys had no part in the battle, a brief account of it serves well to illustrate the spirit and morale of this fighting ship.[2,3]

---

* Belt armour covered certain areas of the sides, protecting boiler and engine rooms and certain other vital spaces.

Late in 1942 *Glasgow* had been attached to the 10th Cruiser Squadron, Home Fleet. In July 1943 she was detached to the Plymouth Command for patrols, with other cruisers, in the Bay of Biscay. On December 27 Coastal Command aircraft reported the approach of a fast German blockade runner, the *Alsterufer*, to the Bay, inbound from Japan. *Glasgow* and other cruisers in the area were ordered to intercept and sink her. The previous day, while *Alsterufer* was about 500 miles west-northwest of Finisterre, a fleet of eleven German destroyers - six Narvik-class and five Elbing-class - left their ports in Brest and Bordeaux to escort her to a Biscay port. Thus, on that last Monday in December two flotillas, each with quite different intentions and each unaware of the other, were steaming at full speed towards the same rendezvous. Neither of them was to make it because aircraft of Coastal Command (or was it surface action by *Ariadne* and *Penelope*, as one account avers?) sank *Alsterufer* while she was yet well west of the rendezvous point.

Other reconnaissance aircraft sighted the destroyers, still steaming westwards, and reported their position to the Admiralty. *Glasgow* and another cruiser, HMS *Enterprise*, were given an easterly course to place them between the outbound Germans and their home ports; with good navigation and a little luck the Germans could be brought to action on their way back home. A little after 0900 on the morning of the 28th, Captain Clarke of *Glasgow* judged that the British ships were now far enough to the east; he altered course to the northwest to intercept the returning enemy.

The cruisers were entering upon a daring encounter. Narvik- class destroyers mounted five 5.9-inch guns; the smaller Elbings were armed with four 4.1-inch guns. In heavy guns alone, the Germans with thirty had the edge over the British, with *Glasgow*'s twelve 6-inch and *Enterprise's* seven 7-inch. Of smaller calibre guns, the Germans had twenty to the British eight. Estimates of the fire power advantage of the Germans have been as high as five to two. Moreover, the Narviks had a five knot speed advantage, and all the destroyers carried a large store of torpedoes. A determined attack by eleven ships from various quarters could well prove fatal to the two cruisers. If either Captain Clarke in *Glasgow* or Captain Grant(RCN) in *Enterprise* had reckoned these sums and weighed the possible consequences, they remained undeterred. The cruisers, their bows casting the rough weather water in white sheets, sped to join battle with the enemy.

At 1100, the destroyers had turned for home, but they had delayed too long; *Glasgow* and *Enterprise*, still below the horizon, were placed to bar their way. At 1313 the cruisers hoisted their battle ensigns; at 1338 they sighted the first German ship; at 1346 *Glasgow* opened fire at 18,000 yards; at 1348 *Enterprise's* first salvoes started from 20,000 yards. The battle had been joined.

In the beginning, the Germans were not cowed. They altered course to engage the British on a roughly parallel southeasterly course, laying smoke to add to the gloom of an already dark afternoon. Soon their fire was straddling the cruisers. For their part, the cruisers had a plethora of targets, and were scoring hits, but the smoke and the poor light made it difficult to assess their effectiveness. Certainly, the German gunnery continued to be accurate. One shell found

*Enterprise*, but did little damage.

Meanwhile, German planes had arrived on the scene. Both British ships had near misses from glider bombs. The cruisers' high angle 4-inch and pom-pom guns soon despatched the bombers, however, and full attention could once more be focused on the destroyers. This renewed attention proved too much for the enemy who altered away northwards in a bid to escape. *Enterprise* would have none of that. Running in, she hit and stopped one destroyer, continuing on to engage two others. They returned heavy and accurate fire, shooting off *Enterprise's* aerial. Then seven German ships broke off the action and steamed north at full speed. The four remaining Germans were in serious trouble. One, heavily damaged, was painfully sneaking away behind a smoke screen. One was stopped and going nowhere. Of the other two, *Glasgow* was engaging one, and Enterprise was slugging it out with the other. By 1600 the cruisers had sunk their opponents; they then sent the stopped destroyer to the bottom.

The early darkness of the late December day was coming on. Visibility was failing; ammunition was running low. The badly damaged destroyer behind her smoke screen was suffered to escape. It had been a pretty good afternoon: one shell hit and assorted minor damage from shrapnel to *Enterprise*; shell splinter damage to *Glasgow* and two ratings killed. On the German side, three destroyers - *Z 27, T 26* and *T 27* - sunk, and many, if not all the remaining eight, variously damaged. Well satisfied with themselves, the two cruisers turned for home.

1. *Naval Historical Branch Papers S 9515 and S 5640.* (London: Imperial War Museum, 1979)

2. Joseph Shull, *The Far Distant Ships.* (Ottawa: Queen's Printer, 1952.) 199 - 202.

3. *Naval Historical Branch Paper S 9515.* (London: Imperial War Museum, 1979)

a).

b).

c).

*a). HMS <u>Glasgow</u> in 1945, after her refit.*
*b). <u>Glasgow</u> in rough weather, 1942. A wartime censor has removed the radar aerials from the picture.*
*c). After the Biscay action. Captain Clarke and his "Number One", Commander Lloyd-Davies.*
*IWM Neg. No. FL2254, FL 4672, unknown.*

## 8. AN RCNVR RATING IN THE ROYAL NAVY.

After breaking off action on December 28, *Glasgow* steamed at best speed for Plymouth, arriving there the following day. The first priority was the further care of the wounded. Their shipmates carefully bore them ashore on stretchers and saw them put in ambulances for transport to hospital. Next came repairing the damage from shell splinters, overhauling the guns and a general restoration of order after the battle. All this was accomplished by January 5; reammunitioned, refuelled and reprovisioned, *Glasgow* was once again in all respects ready for sea.

The RCNVR contingent arrived at Portsmouth from Greenock just as this flurry of activity was beginning. They had a temporary stay in barracks in Portsmouth before they could join the ship, which was at Plymouth. On December 31 a draft, including Vernon and his mates, went on board at about 0200 and found, if not the entire ship's company, at least a number of ratings who would be their future messmates and opposite numbers, up and waiting to welcome them.

One has to know what a precious commodity is sleep for sailors in a warship to appreciate the warmth of such a welcome. At sea, regardless of the watch system in use, no one has the luxury of undisturbed sleep. In harbour, catching up on lost sleep is a high priority, yet here were men who could have been snug in their hammocks up and waiting for the newcomers. It must be remembered, though, that this crew had been together for a long time - some had been in the ship since she was commissioned seven years before - and they were profesionals in the best traditions of the Royal Navy. They probably needed little encouragement from their officers to "put their best foot forward" at this time.

Glasgow's crew was organized to meet the Canadians on a "buddy system" whereby each RCNVR rating was matched to an opposite number ("oppo" in RN slang) from the ship's company. Vernon's oppo was a gunlayer like himself, nicknamed "Scouse"*. Scouse had spaces already reserved where Vernon could sling and stow his hammock. Later, he would even allow Vernon the use of his dhobey bucket, a rare privilege indeed, as a bucket for one's laundry was a highly prized possession, and jealously guarded. Most immediately however, a snack of tea and toast was appropriate. Vernon was fascinated to see his toast being prepared by sandwiching a slice of bread between two hot smoothing irons. Electric toasters were unknown in Scouse's mess!

Indeed, the Canadians expected, and found, many differences in customs and amenities in *Glasgow*, as compared to what they knew in HMC Ships. The mess decks were starker than those in their own navy, and crowded by a wartime complement almost one third larger than the peacetime crew. The prevailing decor was grey steel. Any pretence toward comfort was sacrificed to the working of the guns, whose armoured cylindrical supports, or barbettes, penetrated all

---

In British slang a "Scouser" is a native of the Liverpool/Birkenhead area.

decks. The heads were some distance away in one direction, washing facilities equally far away in another. There was no natural light and little ventilation. The barbette supporting one of the forward turrets passed through the mess deck. The mess tables stood in the midst of machinery; the lockers were jammed in odd corners. On the hammock bars overhead each rating had a space twenty-one inches wide in which to sling his mick.

Coming down from Greenock on the train the Canadians had planned how they would change the way things were done in the Royal Navy. Canadian naval ways, they were convinced, would vastly improve life in ships still bound by Nelsonian traditions; it was simply a matter of showing the Limeys a better way. Of course, their naivete was soon exposed, and all ideas of reforming Royal Naval routine abandoned. In the first place, as their own experience of sea life should have told them, the Navy has its way of doing everything and in most instances, that way having been forged and tested by time and circumstance, it is usually the best, if not the only way. Secondly, the treatment they received on joining the ship won them over completely. From the captain on down, the ship's company of *Glasgow* took them to themselves. "We were", as Vernon recalls, "treated like royalty".

They were not treated so royally as to be exempted for work. After all, they were in this ship for training, and Vernon's training began soon enough. During his first day on board, Vernon was introduced to the inside of a 6-inch gun turret; Scouse had been gunlayer in this turret, but from now on Vernon was to occupy his seat between the middle and the starboard gun. To be shut in this smoothly moving steel enclosure with three guns, their accompanying machinery and crew of twenty-seven, was a far cry from the open gun shields and cranky action of *Prince David's* antiquated cannons. There was a lot to learn.

Scouse explained to Vernon that in most actions the layers and trainers had very little to do, since the aiming of the guns was all done from the Fire Control Centre deep in the ship. In the highest position in the ship, between the mainmast and the bridge, was the Director Tower, manned by the Director Control Officer and several ratings. The heart of the Director was a highpowered range-finding telescope which when properly aimed at the base of an enemy's mainmast, gave the distance of the target and its bearing from *Glasgow*. From repeated observations, the target's course and speed could be estimated. This information was transmitted to the Fire Control Centre where it was fed into a complicated formula which included factors such as *Glasgow's* course and speed, wind direction and velocity, relative humidity of the atmosphere, air temperature, temperature of the guns, wear on the bore of the gun barrels and any other condition which could affect the flight of the shell towards its target. The resolution of this sum, calculated by machine, was translated into the angle of elevation of the guns and their bearing from the ship necessary for the shell to find its target. These settings were sent to the guns electrically, aiming them automatically. The trainer's job was to ensure, by watching a pointer moving with the turret and a pointer moving in response to the Fire Control Centre, that the turret was reacting correctly to instructions from the Centre.

Meanwhile, other members of the guns' crews would have loaded the guns: with the massive breech blocks unlocked and swung open, a shell was rammed in as far as it would go; a cordite charge in its canvas casing was rammed behind the shell; the primer for the charge was set; and the breech slammed shut and locked. All this was accomplished in much less time than it takes to tell about it. The layer's task was to depress the gun (i.e., raise the breech) to the correct height for loading and, when the breech locked shut, to restore the gun to the elevation given from the Fire Control Centre. This done, a bell sounded in the turret, and a "Guns Ready" lamp glowed in the Fire Control Centre and the Director, telling the Gunnery Officer that he could fire when he wished. After firing, the breeches would be swung open and the guns reloaded with shells and charges constantly supplied to the turret by hoists reaching down through the barbette to the magazines at the bottom of the ship. Each turret had three shell hoists and two cordite hoists.

With so many variables in the aiming formula, it was never expected that the first salvo would hit the target, especially at extreme range. Accordingly, observers in the Director tower watched carefully for the splashes indicating the fall of shot. If the splash was beyond the target, the salvo was registered as an "over", and the range was reduced for the next salvo; if the splash was on the near side of the target it was declared a "short", and the range for the next salvo was increased. By a succession of corrections for "overs" and "shorts", salvoes or parts of salvoes should be made to hit the target. In the case of a hit, observers would see no splash, but they might observe a flash from the explosion of the shell on the target or see smoke if a fire was set off. Scoring hits was, of course, the objective, for direct hits caused maximum damage. But "straddles", where shells from a salvo landed close to both sides of the target, were also effective, damaging upperworks and killing or wounding personnel.

All of this was just theory while the ship was in port. It remained for gun drill at sea and/or action against the enemy, really to put Vernon "in the picture". He wondered what it would be like inside the turret, and whether he would perform well. He hadn't long to wait to find out.

On January 14, 1944 *Glasgow* went to sea on a `Special Operation'. Her course was westsouthwesterly into the Atlantic for a day, then southerly for another day. At 1000 on Sunday January 16 she met the battleship *HMS King George V*, escorted by the cruiser *Mauritious*. *Mauritious* detached and *Glasgow* took station on the *"KG V"* at three and a half cables (262 feet) to escort her to Plymouth. The ships reached Plymouth on January 18. *Glasgow* secured, but *KG V* slipped at 1503. The reason for the trip was kept secret because *King George V* was carrying Prime Minister Churchill back from Gibraltar after his meeting earlier in the month with General de Gaulle in Marrakesh.[1] Perhaps the secrecy was not as tight as Their Lordships of the Admiralty might have wished, for Bill O'Neil recalls[2] "we sailed directly behind the K.G.V all the way back and anytime during the day you could see "Winnie" pacing around the quarter deck".

The gun crews were exercised during this trip, as they always were when at sea. Vernon soon became accustomed to the organized confusion inside the turret: the banging of the breech blocks; the shouted orders; the disciplined double-quick actions of the loading and ramming numbers; the clanging of the firing bell; the noise of the guns firing; and the smoke and cordite fumes wafting back from the guns as the breeches opened. It all created, in Vernon's words, "a commotion that kept you occupied", but he was proud and pleased that he was able to play his part in the team working the turret.

Gunnery drills continued while in harbour, alternating with chipping paint and cleaning ship. On February 5 they went to sea for the day to practise gunnery with HMS *Bellona*. On the 9th they were out again for torpedo drill, and lost a torpedo. On February 10, at 0900, *Glasgow* slipped and proceeded at twenty-four knots on a dog leg course west of Biscay to Gibraltar. During the fourteen-hour stay in "Gib", some of the crew, including Vernon, went ashore. Vernon remembers the towering bulk of "The Rock" and of seeing the narrow isthmus towards Spain, but does not recall seeing any of the major fortifications or the famous Barbary apes.

Convoy HK 28A was assembled in Gib and ready to leave for Britain with *Glasgow* as escort. After six days of zigzagging at fifteen knots, convoy and escort parted company off the northern tip of Ireland. The convoy continued around Ireland to Liverpool; Glasgow turned south to Devonport.

Washing down and painting ship occupied the next few days at Devonport and Plymouth Sound. In the Sound, Vernon was a spectator to the comings and goings of destroyers of the 10th Destroyer Flotilla, as they made their nightly sorties in the English Channel. There were several Tribal class ships in the flotilla, including the Canadians HMCS *Haida*, *Huron* and *Athabaskan*. Vernon made a mental note to visit *Athabaskan* at the earliest opportunity, to see his good friend from P.E.I., Murchison Gordon.

On March 5 *Glasgow* left Plymouth carrying a party of RAF personnel to the Azores where, since the previous year, Britain had leased bases from the Portuguese for the anti-submarine war. (Portugal, although neutral, had an ancient treaty with Britain allowing use of the islands in time of war.)

Biscay and the Atlantic were in a good mood, Vernon recalls, and it was a pleasant trip. *Glasgow* anchored off Angra on March 8, disembarked her passengers and moved to anchor off Horta. Shore leave alternated with cleaning ship for both watches on the 9th. The peacetime atmosphere ashore was in marked contrast to their other leaves and was much enjoyed by the sailors.

At 0747 on the 10th *Glasgow* slipped; within minutes she was aground aft. It required several tugs, heaving simultaneously, to haul the ship clear. After a quick inspection by a diver to confirm that no damage had occurred, *Glasgow* was aweigh at 1245. On the 11th, at 1450, *Glasgow* rendezvoused with another inbound fast convoy, which she escorted north. As they rounded Ireland, *Glasgow* worked up speed, passed the convoy and proceeded to Greenock.

On all these trips, gunnery training was continued. When communications between the Fire Control Centre and the turret were working properly, a gunlayer had only to oversee the turret's response to information coming from the Fire Control Centre. If there was an electrical failure, manual laying of the guns was a backup procedure and, of course, the crews were drilled in this.

On one occasion during the Gibraltar trip, the Captain of the turret noticed that Vernon seemed to be following the moving pointers with his finger. He immediately suspected Vernon's eyesight. Accordingly, as soon as the ship returned to port, Vernon was sent to *HMS Drake*, the shore establishment at Plymouth, for eye tests. These tests indicated that his visual acuity was not sharp enough for an LR III. On March 2, 1944, he lost his rating and was reassigned to the crew of a 4-inch anti-aircraft mount as a member of the ammunition supply party. He felt then, and has felt ever since, that he was used unfairly, but in a ship like *Glasgow* even a suspicion of less than 100 per cent efficiency was not tolerated.

*Glasgow* went up to the Clyde on her return from the Azores to be fitted with Plan Position Indicator (PPI), which would further refine the control of her guns. Installation of the new equipment was followed by bombardment exercises on the range at Lamlash, Isle of Arran, for several days until March 26, when the ship returned to Plymouth. Vernon spent the next three weeks helping to clean ship and paint. In one long day the starboard side was freshly painted; the next day the port side was done. On the 11th there was a foray outside for anti-submarine and torpedo trials with *Haida* and *Huron*.

On the evening of March 13 a party of fifteen Americans was embarked. At midmorning the next day, *Glasgow* slipped to return to Greenock. At Greenock Vernon could see, among the many ships riding to buoys in the wide river, the familiar silhouettes of *Prince David* and *Prince Henry*. Although he wondered what brought them here, he had no opportunity of visiting his former ship to find out. An elderly American battleship, USS *Texas* arrived overnight, and at 0830 next morning the cruiser HMS *Belfast* joined them.

*Glasgow* had returned to Greenock for bombardment practice on the range at Kintyre. The Americans who had boarded at Plymouth were a Forward Observation (Bombardment) Party, FOBS for short. They went ashore at Crossaig Bay to call back fall of shot during the bombardment, thus gaining experience themselves and exercising the ship's 6-inch control in communication, ranging and correction. After several days under fire the Americans pronounced themselves impressed and returned on board. Further shoots by all guns and an anti-submarine exercise with HMS *Thorough* were completed before returning to Plymouth. These trials had indicated that all guns were firing short; specialized "boffins" came on board at Plymouth to conduct test firings to get at the root of this problem. By May 6, they had a solution: a new range receiver, connected to the Director, and a modification to the fuse setting machine. Over the next few days test firing validated the changes.

In addition to the cruisers and other warships of the Plymouth Command, ships of the 10th Destroyer Flotilla had been operating out of Plymouth since January. The destroyers, frequently accompanied by a cruiser, were engaged upon two long range programmes: Operation Tunnel, directed against German coastal convoys and their escorts in Biscay and the Channel; and Operation Hostile, a minelaying action against enemy Channel ports, in which the destroyers and cruisers covered the fast minelayers from attack by German ships, including three Elbings berthed at Brest.[3]

Three Canadian Tribal class destroyers, HMCS *Haida*, *Athabaskan* and *Huron*, were attached to the 10th Destroyer Flotilla. By the latter part of April, *Athabaskan* had been on nine patrols on either Tunnel or Hostile missions. Between patrols she went out nightly with other ships of the Flotilla to practise night fighting, navigation, radar detection and radar-controlled gunnery. Although these sorties always had the potential for an encounter with enemy destroyers and/or E-Boats, up until the night of April 25 no contacts had occurred. At 2100 on April 25 the light cruiser HMS *Black Prince*, with the destroyers HMS *Ashanti*, HMCS *Haida*, *Huron* and *Athabaskan* left Plymouth on a Tunnel mission, their destination a position about ten miles off the French coast, seventeen miles ENE of Ile de Bas. Their orders: to intercept and destroy the Elbings, then known to be in St. Malo, should they be so foolish as to leave harbour.

The British force was on station promptly at 0130 on the 26th, and within a half hour *Black Prince* had a radar echo at 21,000 yards, dead ahead. A moment or two later *Ashanti* and *Haida* confirmed the contact. The Germans had come out.

When first detected, the enemy ships were steaming NE at 20 knots, but they must have had their radar sweeping ahead, too, for the British had scarcely plotted their initial course and speed when the ships reversed course and increased to 24 knots. They were running for cover.

*Black Prince* and her hound pack of destroyers increased speed to thirty knots and gave chase. In half an hour they had closed the range to 13,000 yards and the cruiser fired starshell, according to a predetermined strategy. There they were: three German destroyers dead ahead, range five miles. *Huron* and *Athabaskan*, being on *Black Prince's* starboard bow, opened fire first; the other two destroyers opened three minutes later. *Black Prince* continued to fire starshell. The Germans made smoke as they exchanged salvoes with the destroyers. It was an eerie scene: wraiths of greyish-white smoke twisting on the water in the orange-green light of the starshells, and offshore, in the darkness, the flash of the destroyers' 4.7-inch guns, and in the smoke, answering flashes from the Germans. Twelve minutes into the battle, a new light appeared momentarily: a dull red glow marking where one of *Ashanti's* shells bad found its target; five minutes later, another glow told of another hit, but from whose guns it is not known.

The fleeing Elbings were trying to get in amongst the islands dotting the French coast, not only to hide, but to confuse their pursuers' radar, which was already showing a confusion of blips. At 0320 *Haida* could only distinguish two ships on her radar; almost simultaneously observers on *Black Prince* saw a torpedo pass down the port side; one of the enemy had broken away and had very nearly scored big on her tormentors. It was a brave, but not a wise move. Five minutes later *Haida* spotted the Elbing two and a half miles away. Her first salvo hit the German aft. The second and third salvoes went in amidships. Fires broke out in the Elbing even as *Athabaskan's* shells rained in on her, and in a few minutes the German ship was stopped and ablaze from stem to stern. She did not die easily; spurting flames masthead high, she fought on, even though there was no hope. Not until 0421, with all four of her attackers snarling about her, their guns pouring in shells at point blank range, did she sink.

On the morning of April 28, at Plymouth, Vernon got permission to visit his friend and fellow Islander, Murchison Gordon, in *Athabaskan*. "Murky" had been in the Navy a bit longer than Vernon, had seen lots of action and had been mentioned in despatches for quick thinking and bravery in disposing of a potential explosive over his ship's side.

After almost four years in the Navy, the two young sailors had a lot to talk about. First Murky told Vernon about the action in the Channel two nights before. Vernon, who had yet to see action, hung on every detail.They laughed at the thought of *Black Prince's* radar mistaking islands for ships, not appreciating, perhaps, the difficulties of interpreting blips. They discussed the rumours of the big show - The Invasion - which they knew could not be long ahead. They remembered mutual friends in and out of the Service. Best of all, they talked of home, which was so distant, yet seemed so near in their hearts. They might have talked on for who knows how long, but a small air raid over the city and harbour sent Vernon hurrying back to *Glasgow* and his action station on a 4-inch HA. By the time he got there the "All Clear" had sounded. Some bombs had fallen, but no ships were hit. *Glasgow's* A.A. guns had joined in the reception for the German planes, but no hits were observed.

That evening at 2200 *Athabaskan* and *Haida* slipped once more out of Plymouth, bound to protect a flotilla of minelayers near the mouth of the Morlaix River. Shortly before 0300 on the 29th, orders from Plymouth directed the two destroyers SW at full speed to intercept an enemy force moving west close inshore. At 0359 *Athabaskan* made radar contact at 14 miles: at first two echoes, and later three. At 0412, the range having closed to 7,300 yards, *Athabaskan* fired starshell. Two Elbings were revealed; they immediately laid smoke and turned away. Both Canadian ships opened fire, turning as they did so to present their bows to the enemy. German destroyers often fired torpedoes when they turned away, and the narrow beam of a head-on destroyer was a more elusive target than a ship's full length.

*Athabaskan* had just steadied on the new course when a torpedo struck aft, sending a fiery pillar aloft into the night sky. The stricken ship lost way and turned to port, her propellers smashed and her rudder broken. Fires erupted aft and amidships, silencing all the after guns immediately. The forward guns fired on for a little time but soon stopped, too. As the ship began to settle by the stern, the order, "Stand by to abandon" was given, but then hope soared momentarily. A damage control party was making good progress in connecting a seventy ton pump with which to fight the worst of the fires, but as it turned out, their efforts were in vain. Even as the last connections of the pump were completed, the racing fire reached the magazine. When the ammunition exploded, the column of flame and smoke was seen thirty miles away.

*Haida* was hotly engaged with an Elbing that she had already damaged; she pressed the attack until the German destroyer was driven, blazing furiously, onto the rocks. The other Elbing had escaped, so with heavy heart, *Haida* returned to the survivors of *Athabaskan*. They were barely five miles offshore, within range of shore batteries and a tempting target for aircraft. For all that, *Haida* stopped for fifteen minutes with scramble nets over the side; thirty-eight survivors came on board. She had also lowered her motor boat, but when the widening dawn forced her to leave, the boat and its crew were left behind with the rest of the survivors.

Daylight brought three German minesweepers out to make prisoners of the remaining survivors. L/S W.A. McLure, coxswain of the motor boat, was not going to be a prisoner if he could help it. With his crew of two and eight survivors, he set course for a cross-channel voyage. In the early evening they were spotted by RAF Spitfires who directed rescue craft to their position. Altogether, forty-four Athabaskans were rescued; eighty-three were made prisoners of war; the captain and 127 of the ship's company died off the French coast that tragic night. Murchison Gordon was one of them. The Navy mourned the loss of a fine ship and a gallant ship's company; Vernon grieved for the death of a good friend.

It seemed unlikely that the torpedo came from the Elbings; the radar had shown three blips, but there were only two ships in the light of the starshell. Was that third echo from an E-Boat which, outside the illumination of the starshell, took fatal aim at Athabaskan? The question was unresolved until after the war, when German records became available. According to them, the three destroyers out on the night of April 25 were *T 24*, *T 27* and *T 29*. The latter was Haida's and Huron's victim. On the night of April 28/29, *T 24* and *T 27* were out again. In the deadly tit for tat that night, Haida got *T 27* and a torpedo from *T 24* sank Athabaskan. In another of war's cruel ironies, it had not even been properly aimed.[4] While turning away, *T 24* had launched a spread of six torpedoes in the general direction of the Canadian ships. Half of the torpedoes went one way, half of them went in the opposite direction. One of the wanderers found *Athabaskan*.

That third blip on the radar screen? Who knows?

1. Peter Simkins. *Imperial War Museum Memo* to the *Director General, July 6,1997.* Copied to Lawson Drake.

2. Bill O.Neil. *Personal communication* to *Lawson Drake, February, 1999.*

3. Joseph Shull, *The Far Distant Ships.* (Ottawa: Queen's Printer, 1952) 250 - 258

4. Alan D. Butcher, *I Remember Haida* (Hanysport, Nova Scotia: Lancelot Press, 1985) 59 - 60

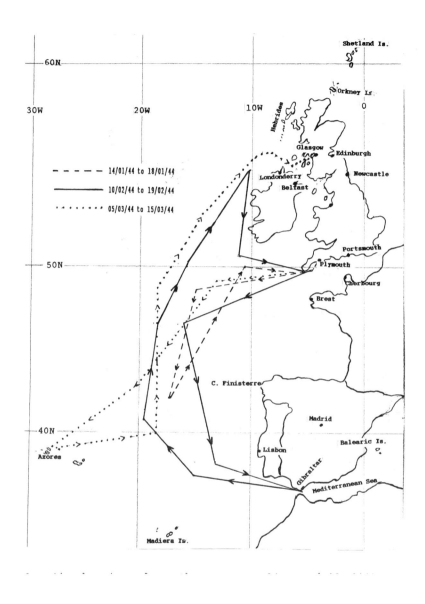

*Operational cruises of <u>HMS Glasgow</u> January 14 - March 15, 1944.*

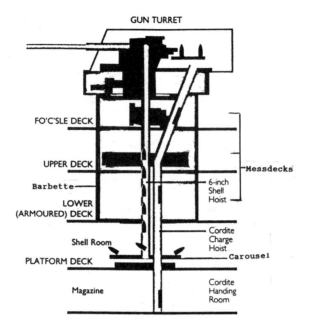

GUN TURRET

FO'C'SLE DECK

UPPER DECK

Messdecks

Barbette

6-inch
Shell
Hoist

LOWER
(ARMOURED) DECK

Cordite
Charge
Hoist

Shell Room

PLATFORM DECK

Carousel

Magazine

Cordite
Handing
Room

a).

*a). Vertical section through a cruiser's triple 6-inch turret and ring bulkhead (barbette), showing ammunition supply. Total weight of the structure was about 160 tons.*
*b). Interior of a 6-inch turret. Centre gun (on left of photo) breech is open with 100-pound projectile on the tray ready for ramming. Starboard gun (right of photo) has had projectile loaded; the cordite charge is on the tray, ready for ramming.*

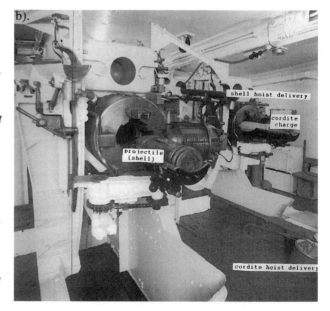

b).

shell hoist delivery

cordite
charge

projectile
(shell)

cordite hoist delivery

# 9. BATTLE HONOUR: NORMANDY.

There was a feeling in the messdecks and the wardroom that *Glasgow* was being prepared for something big. And little wonder: the emphasis on bombardment training was something new; and there was an urgency about Plymouth in April and May of 1944. The port was busy with ships - both warships and merchantmen. Square-stemmed, open decked vessels, clearly intended as assault landing craft, occupied camouflaged berths all around the harbour. The most persistent rumour - a cross Channel invasion - gained credence when, early on May 4, *Glasgow*, with *Haida* and USS *Augusta,* left Plymouth for Slapton Sands to participate in Operation Fabius I, a full scale rehearsal of an amphibious assault. This exercise was so realistic that, in Vernon's memory, it is merged with his recollections of the actual invasion a month later. The details recounted here come largely from Colin Balfour's Midshipman's Log[1]

At dawn, landing craft and support craft took their appointed positions offshore. *Glasgow's* 6-inch guns began firing with live ammunition at 0650. The spotter reported the first salvo landing 3,000 yards off target, but the correct range was soon found and *Glasgow* happily banged off the remainder of her 50 rounds on target. Meanwhile, planes of the RAF and USAAF strafed and bombed the beaches ahead of the infantry who went in precisely at 0730.

With the troops ashore, *Glasgow* moved closer in to receive simulated calls for supporting fire. The weather worsening in the afternoon, *Glasgow* assisted in "mothering" the other ships until she withdrew for Plymouth at 1600. It had been a very realistic exercise, the more so as a stick of badly aimed bombs from a Marauder narrowly missed *Glasgow* astern. No one now doubted what was ahead; the questions now were, "When?" and "Where?".

In the days following Fabius, preparations for the real thing intensified: 6-inch gun control and communications were rigorously rehearsed; guns of all calibers were exercised against aircraft, sleeve and surface targets. Vernon's action station was on a 4-inch HA mount, and he remembers that when a Hurricane pilot, whose aircraft was a "live" target for these guns , was asked to comment on the accuracy of their fire, his reply was, "Too bloody accurate". Colin Balfour relates that when this exercise was ended the Hurricane, flaps and undercarriage down, flew slowly up *Glasgow's* port side at bridge level "making what we hoped was a`V-for-Victory' sign as he passed." Damage control parties were drilled in various emergency procedures; towing routines were rehearsed. Four additional Oerlikons (20mm cannons) were mounted. The First Motor Boat, all the spare torpedoes and considerable wooden furniture were removed to storage ashore. They would not be required in the days ahead; in the ship they were fire and explosion hazards.

During May, some of *Glasgow's* crew, including Vernon, got four days' leave. A shipmate invited Vernon to come with him to his sister's home in Worthing. Together, they made the short trip to the pleasant seaside town through a part of England where invasion preparations were already in progress. Vernon remembers warm spring days, relaxation and lots of lamb stew. Spring would be over, and summer well advanced before there would be any more relaxation or the prospect of home-cooked food.

Shortly after their return to the ship - May 22 at 1632, to be exact - *Glasgow* sailed for Belfast, accompanied by the destroyers HMS *Vimy* and *Vesper* as screen. Rounding Land's End, the little flotilla plowed north through St. George's Channel into the Irish Sea. Leaving the screen behind, *Glasgow* arrived at Belfast Lough to secure to a buoy at 1350, May 23. The Lough was crowded with shipping of many nationalities - American, French, Polish and Canadian, to name just a few.

At least some people in *Glasgow* knew now what was afoot. "We knew it was coming about a fortnight before; tension was growing, movements increasing - and then we sailed for our assembly points." So that was it: *Glasgow* was in Belfast Lough to join the fleet that was to support the thousands of assault troops set to invade the continent. That fleet was to be so huge that it could not be assembled in any one harbour; moreover, dispersal would help to keep the enemy from correctly guessing the Allied plans.

Accordingly, ships were despatched to various assembly areas within a day or two's steaming of the coast of France to form up with their battle groups and wait for the order that would commit them to the invasion.

Vernon did not recognize any old friends among the warships already anchored in, or arriving at, Belfast Lough, but among them were a number who would be new friends before long. The cruisers HMS *Hawkins* and *Enterprise* were there, as were the battleships USS *Texas, Arkansas* and *Nevada*. The American ships were veterans, older than most of the sailors in that harbour, having been part of the American Naval Squadron which came to Europe late in World War I; some had participated in amphibious landings in the Pacific in this war. There were a number of American cruisers, including USS *Quincy* (which would shortly have the honour of being inspected by the Supreme Commander, General Eisenhower). There were destroyers too numerous to name, and still smaller ships - frigates and corvettes. Among them were several ships of the RCN.*

A novel sight was two French cruisers, the *Georges Leygues* (to Vernon and the other ratings she was soon known as "Georgie's Legs") and the *Montcalm*. Their voyage to Belfast Lough had been long and circuitous, politically speaking. At the fall of France in 1940 they were in Toulon where they came under control of the Vichy regime. On September 10, 1940, with another cruiser and some destroyers, they broke out from Toulon in a dash for Dakar on the west African coast. They were sighted by RN ships at 0515 next morning 50 miles east of Gibraltar but owing to a mixup in signals they eluded the Royal Navy and escaped through the Straits to the open Atlantic. Later that month, during the abortive British attack on Dakar, they traded salvoes with RN ships. Even when Dakar surrendered to the Allies on November 23, 1942, they refused to come onside. Only when the conquest of North Africa was complete did these

---

* For a list of RCN ships paricipating in the Normandy invasion, see Appendix A.

ships rally to the cause as Free French ships.[3] Now they lay in Belfast Lough waiting to return to France.

The next week was spent in daily trips to sea to practise signalling, taking position for bombarding, gunnery control for all calibers and so on. In harbour the crew was rotated off for afternoon leaves, but on May 30 *Glasgow* was sealed. Shore leave was stopped; mails were cancelled. The ship's company was effectively cut off from all communication with the shore. Now the Captain could open his orders and learn what role his ship was to play in the great drama ahead. Having done that, Captain Clarke ordered lower decks cleared and spoke to his ship's company over the public address system. *Glasgow*, he said, was to participate in Operation Neptune, the naval part of Operation Overlord, the invasion of Nazi-occupied Europe. They would be part of Bombarding Force C, operating in support of Assault Force C comprising American troops which were to land on the coast of France between Vierville and Port en Bessin. The assault beach was code-named "Omaha".

They were to be the only RN ship in this force, which would include *Texas, Arkansas, Georges Leygues, Montcalm* and *Augusta*, Admiral Hall's (USN) flagship. *Quincy* would be there, with USS *Tuscaloosa* and *Nevada*, HMS *Enterprise* and *Black Prince*, but they were part of another force, assigned to another beach. *Glasgow* had pride of place; she would lead the heavy ships in, behind the minesweepers and destroyers.

The Captain spoke with utter confidence of success in the coming operation. He described the build-up of men and equipment in preparation for the attack, amazing Vernon as he told of the thousands of ships and planes and the tens of thousands of soldiers soon to go into battle. It was, he said, the beginning of the end of the war in Europe.

Next day the Gunnery Officer took up the story in more detail. *Glasgow* was to get in close to shore, he explained, navigating through a narrow channel swept free of mines to an anchorage from which her guns would fire on shore targets. The first of these was certain coastal defense batteries whose positions had already been pinpointed. After these had been dealt with, the guns would be turned on other targets - enemy observation posts, troop concentrations, tanks, etc., picked out by the troops ashore or by the spotter aircraft which would also relay back to them their fall of shot. "Guns",* too, radiated confidence. Given the correct map coordinates for any target, he said, *Glasgow's* 6-inchers would make short work of it. Meanwhile, the 4-inch guns (one of them was Vernon's Action Station) and the pom-poms would be ready to repel any enemy aircraft attacking the fleet. So that everyone might understand as much as possible about what was ahead, they were told to study the maps and scale model of the Normandy coast set up in the hangar. Vernon dutifully looked over the model, but his thoughts turned more on the Luftwaffe than the beaches.

Time for study was getting short. Further preparations for battle were com-

---

* Naval common usage for Gunnery Officer.

pleted: more stores were landed; lifelines were rigged on the upper decks; cabins and messdecks were stripped of tables and other flammables. Vernon and others who had not yet been under fire wondered about what was coming.

*Glasgow* put to sea at 0830 on June 3, in company with the other cruisers - *Tuscaloosa* ahead, *Bellona, Enterprise, Hawkins, Quincy* and *Black Prince* astern - and destroyers, several hours behind the American heavy squadron. The crew was eager and expectant, their spirits buoyed by the confidence of their officers. The hangar displays got a lot of attention as the flotilla moved southwards at fifteen knots. During the day the wind increased and the sky darkened. At 0100 June 4, the ships were cruising slowly through the Irish Sea, biding time so as to reach the French coast early on the morning of the 5th. By 0800 they were off St. Anthony's Head, near Point X, in very rough water, when the captain announced a signal advising a twenty-four hour delay. With disappointed crews, the ships turned back to the Bristol Channel to wait out the storm. There were a lot of ships to be avoided; watchkeepers had to be vigilant.

On the morning of June 5 they were back at position X, in the English channel, steaming in a falling wind, with bright sunshine and intermittent cloud. *Texas* was in the lead, followed by *Glasgow, Arkansas, George Leygues* and *Montcalm*. There were ships everywhere; overhead an umbrella of aircraft flew in their special black and white markings. The Commander spoke, telling the crew where the various assault forces were going in: the British and Canadians on the left; the Americans on the right; 10,000 paratroops to be dropped inland ahead of the seaborne troops. As the Commander spoke, landing craft and vessels of every description came out of the small Channel ports to join the swelling armada. It was like a scene from the Pied Piper as the smaller craft, each with a tethered barrage balloon overhead, took station on the slowly moving convoys.

By now, the initial euphoria was giving way to sober reality. There were ships by the hundreds, as far as the eye could see. How could this great fleet remain undetected? And if and when discovered, then what? Vernon could only speculate.

*Glasgow* went to Action Stations at 2000, before dusk. Remaining mess tables were stowed, offices and cabins cleared. The battle pennant which had last flown in the Biscay action six months before was hoisted. On that occasion it had streamed in the wind of *Glasgow's* own making as she went full ahead to engage the enemy; now at just a few knots headway, *Glasgow* was moving little air, and the battle flag flew on the Channel winds. Gun crews went to First Degree of Readiness, where they were to stay for five days. This meant wearing anti-flash clothing, lifebelts and steel helmets, sleeping by the guns (never mind the steel decks or the steel rivets) and eating by the guns (soup and sandwiches if it was quiet; an energising tablet from tinned "action rations" if it was not). Vernon's station was on the ammunition supply to a twin 4-inch. For him and for the gunners, it promised to be a long night, as it did also for the officers who had to keep perfect station in the midst of a blacked-out fleet. It was eerily quiet.

By early morning, they were in their swept lane, very conscious of *Quincy* coming up astern, and behind her, *Texas*. Once, and once only, *Glasgow* went slightly off course, and had to go astern in the path of the oncoming American cruiser. It was a tense moment which passed quickly. Now, as *Glasgow* felt her way along the swept channel, the Padre came on the P/A to read Nelson's Prayer Before Battle, composed in the early morning before Trafalgar:

*May the Great God, whom I worship, grant to my Country, and for the benefit of Europe in general, a great and glorious Victory; and may no misconduct in any one tarnish it; and may humanity after Victory be the predominant feature in the British Fleet. For myself, individually, I commit my life to Him who made me, and may his blessing light upon my endeavours for serving my country faithfully. To Him I resign myself and the just cause which is entrusted me to defend. Amen Amen Amen.*[4]

To the great Admiral's prayer were added from hearts full of thoughts of home and loved ones, many equally fervent, if less eloquent, private petitions as the long night wore on.

The Navies' role in the invasion of Normandy was code-named "Operation Neptune". In a sense, however, navies contributed much more to the invasion than being present off the beaches on D-Day. Much of the material for the invasion - tanks, trucks, jeeps, guns, ammunition, fuel, landing craft and all manner of miscellaneous supplies from shovels to cigarettes to condoms (widely used as waterproofing for rifle muzzles, rations, matches, etc.) had been convoyed across the Atlantic under the protection of RCN and RN ships. The Canadian and American soldiers also came to Britain in ships, but troopships frequently travelled alone, depending on their speed, isolation and obscure routing for safe passage.

All these naval efforts were history on the grey morning of June 6, 1944. History, too, were the months and years the troops had spent waiting, training, preparing for and anticipating this strike which would be the beginning of the end of the Nazi occupation of Europe. They had done their last battle exercise; they had received their final briefings; they had left their sealed camps and boarded their transports; now, alone with thoughts not to be shared with anyone, they awaited H-Hour.

Every participant in the historic event had been briefed about his own particular role, as well as being told more or less of the overall plan. The operation was so vast, however, that no individual could observe more than a tiny fraction; the many excellent and gripping accounts of that day are collections of the memories of hundreds of survivors.[5]

One common and abiding impression was shared by every person present at D-Day - the great mass of ships. Sailors on the warships, like Vernon and Bill O'Neil in *Glasgow*, and Dick Curley in *Belfast;* the attacking troops; the German defenders; civilian observers ashore and afloat - all remarked on the great mass of boats. "As far as the eye could see was ships", Vernon recalled. "Boats, boats and more boats..." was what a French civilian ashore saw at first light. There were the warships, from battleships to minesweepers; there were transports, blockships, landing ships and landing craft - 6,000 of them all told, crowding into the Bay of the Seine before dawn that June morning.

This great fleet was no milling mass of ships but a tightly organized, disciplined armada, in which each unit had an assigned station and a specific task. Here or there a ship might be out of place, but in the main every ship was where it should be, which was a minor miracle, considering the weather of the past couple of days and the logistics of assembling this fleet. From Falmouth in the west to Newhaven in the east, ships had weighed and sailed from English seaports in a designated sequence, their initial destination Point Z, a circular patch of sea, five miles in diameter, thirteen miles south-east of the Isle of Wight.

From Point Z, more familiarly known as Piccadilly Circus, the fleet was to approach the French coast by ten narrow lanes swept through the German coastal minefields. So the minesweepers, 225 of them, were the vanguard of the fleet. A flotilla was assigned to sweep each lane, the little ships following astern of one another, with their sweeping gear streamed abeam so that the ship ahead cleared a path for the next astern. A wooden-hulled sweeper, proof against magnetic mines, led each flotilla towards shore. At the end of the staggered column a guard ship set out dimly lit dan buoys to mark the edges of the swept channel for the ships that would follow. Timing was crucial; there could be no delay, for the first of the following ships would be well into the swept channels before the minesweepers had completed their tasks.

By 0303 the lanes to the shore had been cleared. The sweepers turned parallel to the coast to clear the onshore waters to ensure the transports safe anchorages and the landing craft clear passage to shore. An international trio of destroyers escorted the sweepers in this work. The Polish ship *Slazak* led the trio in, followed by HMS *Middleton*, with the Norwegian ship *Svenner* in the rear. They were to respond to enemy shore batteries if they fired on the sweepers, but the German guns did not yet speak.

The swept lanes immediately filled with the bombardment fleet feeling its way to anchorages three to fourteen miles offshore. The ships would probably have preferred to remain under way but the narrowness of the swept channels and the congestion of traffic which would develop as the landing forces moved in demanded that they be stationary. The five battleships anchored farthest out. Three were the Americans: USS *Nevada, Texas* and *Arkansas*, on the right with Force C. The other two were British: HMS *Warspite* and *Ramillies*. They were on the left, in support of the British and Canadians. All were seasoned veterans; indeed, they were among the oldest capital ships in their respective fleets. The American ships, as noted earlier, had been part of the US Battle Squadron in these waters late in World War I; *Warspite* at twenty-nine years old, and *Ramillies* at twenty-seven, had also seen action in the First War. They were chosen for their task this day for two reasons: their great guns - from 16-inch in *Texas* to 12-inch in *Arkansas*; and their age (*Arkansas* was the senior, at age thirty-two), because of which they were considered expendable.

Twenty cruisers, including HMS *Glasgow* and HMS *Belfast*, eased to positions closer inshore. Ahead of them, finding their positions nearest the shore was the main destroyer force of sixty-five ships, thirty-one from the USN and thirty-four from the RN and RCN.

The landing beaches, from west to east along the coast of the Bay of the Seine, were Utah, Omaha, Gold, Juno and Sword. The assaulting forces were, by and large, assigned by nation to particular landing zones: Americans to Utah and Omaha; British to Gold and Sword; Canadians to Juno. The same national distinctions were not observed in the bombarding forces, however. *Glasgow* was with *Texas* off Omaha beach. *Texas'* big guns were ranged on Pointe du Hoc; *Glasgow* was to engage a strong point at Les Moulins, near Vierville-sur-Mer, on the beach to the east of Pointe du Hoc. USS *Nevada*, with the cruisers HMS *Black Prince*, USS *Quincy* and *Tuscaloosa* were off Utah, securing the right flank of the assault against a possible German naval response from Cherbourg. Away to the east, off Sword beach, the RN battleships, with a gaggle of cruisers, secured the left flank of Neptune against possible naval attacks out of Le Havre or Ouistreham.

To the planners of Neptune, the threat of German counterattack by sea was quite real. Intelligence reports indicated that the enemy had some 230 surface ships - armed trawlers, E-boats, R-boats and destroyers - at his disposal. Having met these forces in what has since become known as the Battle of the Narrow Seas, the Navy had a healthy respect for their dash and firepower; only weeks before, they had claimed HMCS *Athabaskan*. Although this small German fleet could not defeat the invasion forces, a determined attack pressed against the massed ships could create great havoc and confusion, even perhaps disrupting the delicate timetable of ships' movements during the critical first hours of the landing.

Naval commanders had an additional worry. They estimated that the Germans could concentrate 130 to 200 U-boats from their ports on Biscay, the English Channel and the North Sea on the invasion site within a few days. Patrols of various types of craft - MTB's corvettes, frigates and destroyers - were deployed in the Channel well to the east and west of the landing beaches to counter this perceived U-boat menace.

As it turned out, the German Navy stayed in port on D-Day, except for two sorties by E-boats from Le Havre. The first, at 0348, never reached the main fleet, but boats of the second group penetrated the protective screen to torpedo *Svenner*, destroying her in a spectacular explosion. But *Warspite*, like an old lioness turning on jackals, ranged her guns on the marauders and they were not seen again. Over to the west, two minutes before *Svenner* was hit, German shore batteries opened fire with their 210mm (8.4-inch) guns. In short order *Nevada* was straddled twenty-seven times, but not hit directly. Such were the preliminaries to the main event about to be staged.

American and British air forces had begun bombing Omaha beach about 0130, June 6. A half hour later, from eleven miles offshore, observers on *Glasgow,* watching the spectacle through turret periscopes, could see soaring flames mixed with ascending tracers and descending flares. Vernon had never seen such a display of fireworks. It reminded some of the English lads of the Blackpool illuminations.

Slowly, infinitely carefully, *Glasgow* continued to lead the way in. At 0430, shortly after a lull in the bombing, she came to her anchorage about 4 miles off St. Laurent. The anchor was let go as silently as possible, although it must have mattered little in the building din of exploding bombs how much noise it made. In the breaking dawn, all around *Glasgow*, seaward as far as the eye could see and landward to the shore shrouded in mist and smoke, was a mass of ships - warships of all sizes, transports and landing ships. The preliminaries were almost finished; the main event was about to open.

At his action station on the 4-inch Vernon knew none of the details recorded here. No rating, and few officers, would have a complete picture of the day's events - targets engaged, time of engagement and rounds fired. These are facts gleaned from various accounts, principally *Glasgow's* log book. They are recounted here to give the reader some idea of what this momentous action was like for Vernon and naval participants like him.

For his part, Vernon remembers feeling very tense, and being greatly relieved when, at 0554 all twelve of *Glasgow's* 6-inch guns opened fire, Y turret firing first. When turrets fired simultaneously, the ship shuddered from the recoil.

The targets were shore batteries and smoke mortars in the vicinity of Les Moulins. Off to port, the French cruisers let fly at their targets. Before long the spotting airplane was reporting, "Good shooting!" Simultaneously, landing craft loaded with tanks and troops passed the ship on their way to the shore. At 0615 *Texas* opened fire. Vernon heard her 16-inch shells arching over *Glasgow* with a noise like a freight train, on their way to wreak havoc on Pointe du Hoc.

H-Hour was set for 0620, but the troops were a bit late, and some of them off course. *Glasgow* ceased firing at 0627, resumed at 0634 and checked again at 0640. The rear turret doors were opened to clear the cordite fumes. From the more exposed 4-inch mountings, looking shorewards the guns' crews saw smoke and huge explosions and milling boat traffic close inshore.

Firing resumed at 0804 against vehicles, tanks and gun batteries harassing the landing forces. Again the results were excellent, some targets requiring but one salvo. Intermittent firing went on until 1101, followed by a lull until 1459, after which there was on-again, off-again firing against the village of Trevieres, a road junction four miles inland from St. Laurent. The Torpedo Officer's writer* had vacationed for several peacetime summers in and around Vierville. He spent the day on the bridge where he was considerable help to the Navigator in identifying landmarks.[6] At 1900 there was an urgent call from the beach to engage mobile A.A. guns firing on beach positions, but the guns were too mobile, there was no spotter, and *Glasgow* could not find the range. Firing ceased for the day at 1959. Ten targets had been engaged since dawn.

During that long day Vernon and the others on *Glasgow's* anti-aircraft guns wondered how it was going on the beach. They could see that boat traffic was

---

* A specialized rating trained in clerical work.

being held up, and they were aware that landing craft were being destroyed. They realized that men were dying in there, but none of them had any idea of the full extent of the horror facing the men of the 1st and 29th American Divisions on this heavily defended shore. There had been so much bombing and shelling that it seemed incomprehensible that the Germans could make an effective resistance. By noon the B.B.C.* was telling them that the Canadian landings had gone well, but that the Rangers were still held up on Omaha. From the ship, Pointe du Hoc appeared to have crumbled into the sea; they couldn't know how many American Rangers died scaling that blasted promontory, only to find that the enemy guns were not there, but a half mile farther inland. It would be weeks or months or years later before many of *Glasgow's* crew watching that day would know how narrow was the margin of American success on Omaha beach, and how dearly it cost.

By 1900 it was clear that the troops had advanced inland, leaving a beach strewn with burnt out and burning vehicles and crowded with the dead and wounded. All day the sky had been full of Allied aircraft, identifiable by their black and white striping, but no Luftwaffe appeared. The A.A. gunners, Vernon included, were closed up all day but no hostile aircraft approached their area until 2300. The Americans banged away quite noisily, but as no planes came near *Glasgow*, she held her fire. At 2330 bombs fell near *Glasgow* amid a chorus of ack-ack, but again, lacking an identifiable target, her guns remained silent.

So "the longest day" ended for HMS *Glasgow* and all in her. It had begun with the silent approach to the shore, built up to the crescendo of the bombardment, continued intermittently noisy all day, and ended on a diminuendo of coughing Bofors and chattering Oerlikons. Would there be a quiet time, would there be the composure, for sleep?

Thanks to Allied air superiority and vigilant naval patrols on the flanks of the fleet, enemy aircraft and E-boats were more of a nuisance than a danger during the remaining darkness. Vernon expected air attacks; anti-aircraft crews stood to from 0200 until 0420, losing their sleep, but no attack came.

At 0659 the 6-inch guns resumed firing for the day with a barrage against multi-barrelled mortars that were harassing the troops ashore; soon the spotter was reporting, "Good shooting". About 0800 the anchorage came under fire from the shore. Fire was returned; the ship was moved to another anchorage. At 0925 the road junction at Trevieres, where German tanks and infantry were massing, was shelled again, but with unknown effect. Firing against Trevieres continued until 0952; after a ten minute lull the mortar position was blasted again for thirteen minutes. Firing against Trevieres was resumed at 1042, more enemy having entered the village, and continued for twenty minutes. By the final cease fire at 2125 on D+1, *Glasgow* had engaged thirteen targets. Her guns had destroyed a battery and its ammunition dump, taken out an observation post in a church spire, and broken up numerous troop concentrations - a good day's work. Again, it had been a slack day for the 4-inch crews.

---

* The British Broadcasting Corporation (the "wireless") from London.

The pattern of *Glasgow's* activities for D+2 (June 8) was similar: sporadic firings lasting a few minutes interspersed with periods of inactivity. Eight targets were engaged. As day followed day, the names of the villages they shelled became familiar to the guns' crews: Trevieres, St. Laurent, Vierville and Isigny.

Each day at 0900, the Commander made a situation report to the ship's company. After describing the action in their sector, and summarizing the progress of the ground forces in the other sectors, he took pains to reassure the ship's company that their efforts were contributing to the successes ashore. It was important for the crew to hear this, for they could not see their targets and did not know the effect of their shelling.

During lulls in the action Vernon caught glimpses of what was going on around them. On D+1 he saw the continuing waves of Allied bombers overhead, the reinforcements piling ashore and the arrival of the first of the concrete caissons and blockships which were to be sunk to form the "Mulberry", or temporary harbour, off St. Laurent. On D+4 he watched these components being sunk and the artificial port taking shape.

As American infantry got the measure of the Germans behind the beaches, the names of liberated villages were struck off *Glasgow's* list of targets. Vierville and St. Laurent were the first to go, on D+1; Isigny went on D+2, Trevieres on D+4. As the battle front moved inland, activities on *Glasgow* slowed. The night of June 8 was quiet, and there were no calls for fire on June 9 or 10. Although they remained closed up, Vernon and the 4-inch gun crews snatched some sleep in relays. During the days enemy shore batteries fired on the ships once or twice in a discouraged sort of way. When *Glasgow* appeared to be their target the ship was moved to another anchorage.

The night of June 10/11 was also quiet. Despite the lack of action the guns' crews could not be stood down; everyone in the ship was becoming tired and bored. On the morning of June 10 the Commander allowed an easing in First Degree readiness: henceforth, hands could go to meals in their messdecks so long as two turrets remained closed up for action. Y Gun's crew even played a makeshift game of soccer on the quarterdeck that afternoon, using the top of a cordite case for a ball.

At 2200 on the 10th the Captain spoke: "We will leave here for Portsmouth at 0700 tomorrow". Joy in the messdecks! The mood of the whole ship lifted; the prospect of hard work ammunitioning ship was as nothing compared to thoughts of getting mail, having a bath and spending an uninterrupted night in one's hammock. By 0800 on June 11 *Glasgow* was steaming homewards against an endless procession of ships and aircraft bound for France and the buildup of the forces now well established inland.

In Portsmouth, ammunitioning was completed in four hours and a half; the crew did laundry and had their first baths in six days. And they had their night's sleep. At 0800 on June 12, *Glasgow* cleared Portsmouth on her way back to France. She had on board the headquarters staff of the Second British Army, which she transferred to the destroyer *Hilary* off Courseulles at noon before proceeding to her anchorage off Isigny.

This was *Glasgow's* (and Vernon's) only visit to the eastern sector of the Invasion beaches. An old friend of Vernon's, and some of *Glasgow's* old friends had been there before them, on D-Day. Vernon's old friend was HMCS *Prince David*, in her new life as an Infantry Landing Ship. She had brought 555 officers and men of the Chaudiere Regiment and the Royal Marine Commando to Juno Beach on D-Day. *Glasgow's* old friends were HMS *Belfast* and a number of other cruisers in the bombarding force off Gold and Juno beaches.

Back at her anchorage off Isigny, *Glasgow* learned that in the short space of a day the war beyond Omaha beach had moved out of range of her guns. The last holdout on her list of targets - Carentan - was captured this date, the hard-fighting German paratroops there having finally been overcome. The way for a link-up between the Utah and Omaha beachheads was now cleared; there was nothing more for *Glasgow* to do here. The Commander spoke at 1600, falling out the 6-inch turrets. The ship reverted to normal sea routine until called upon to bombard or to repel aircraft.

The night of June 12/13 was free of alarms. At 1600 on the 13th *Glasgow* moved westwards towards the Cherbourg peninsula, where she joined up with USS *Texas* and other ships, including *Enterprise* and *Quincy*. Some aircraft came over the next morning at 0005 bringing the A.A. crews to Action Stations, but there was no firing.

On D+8 (June 14) the American IVth Division troops began their advance on Cherbourg[7]. The port city was heavily defended against attack from land and sea, and its German commander, Lieut. General von Schlieben, was under fight-to-the-death orders from Hitler. On this morning, as American ground forces moved westwards from Carentan, Allied naval forces began an attack from the sea. At 0700 on June 15 *Glasgow*, with USS *Texas*, HMS *Enterprise* and others, shelled troop concentrations from about a mile offshore at Grandcamp. For the next two days, *Glasgow* returned to "complete and utter boredom"[8] in anchorages off Isigny or St Vaast.

It was not totally boring for everyone. That portion of the 60 block ships and 146 caissons assigned to the St.Laurent Mulberry was in place and Vernon was fascinated to see the engineers completing the pierheads, putting the finishing touches on the floating breakwaters, and laying the miles of floating road-ways connecting the docks to shore. Two days later, late in the afternoon, the first LST tied up at the Mulberry to discharge cargo. It seemed that the slow and labourious task of landing supplies over the beach was ended. The Channel weather, however, was to have the final word on that issue. Never really settled since D-Day, it turned downright fierce on June 19. A full gale blowing out of the north-east wrecked the St.Laurent Mulberry beyond repair[9]. Fortunately, Mulberry B, the British Mulberry at Arromanches, survived the storm and gave invaluable service until captured Channel ports could be made usable.

During June 18, 19 and 20 *Glasgow* fired on a number of targets along the east coast of the Cotentin peninsula. Return fire from the shore was light and quickly silenced. Daily minesweeping was still necessary to clear mines laid dur-ing the nights, but air alerts were becoming increasingly rare. On the 19th, during the storm, the ship was off St. Vaast-la-Hogue. Vernon could see towering columns of flame along the waterfront, but next day, as the gale subsided, watchers on the ship got the impression of green, peaceful, rolling countryside and undamaged villages.

St. Vaast was the eastern anchor of a line of forts placed five or six miles south of Cherbourg in a protective semicircle around the city. Along the east coast north of St.Vaast, farther north at Barfleur, and at Fermanville on the north coast near Cherbourg itself, the Germans had sited heavy coastal batteries. At least fifteen of the twenty batteries were 150mm calibre or greater, including three 280mm (11.2 inch). The guns were emplaced in massive blockhouses of reinforced concrete immune to high explosive shells. A lucky hit on the open gunports was the only hope of silencing them. As the infantry fought its way to the outer defences of the city, the bombarding fleet addressed itself to the problem of these shore batteries.

On June 22 *Glasgow* withdrew to Portsmouth for ammunition, fuel and supplies. Meanwhile four squadrons of RAF Typhoons, six squadrons of Mustangs and 375 US fighter-bombers plastered the defenses of Cherbourg with rockets and bombs. *Glasgow* returned to the peninsula on the morning of June 25, going to Action Stations at 0800. She was part of Group 1, Task Force 129, comprising USS *Nevada, Tuscaloosa, Quincy* and HMS *Enterprise*, six U.S. destroyers (USS *Hambledon, Rodman, Emmons, Murphy, Gherardi* and *Ellyson*), a flotilla of minesweepers and some MLs. Under the command of Rear Admiral Morton Deyo USN, in *Tuscaloosa*, they were going to take on the coastal batteries.[10]

The morning was sunny, the sea calm. The minesweepers had cleared a path to within about 13,000 yards of shore when the Germans opened up. Their aim was right on, imperilling the sweepers; the MLs hastened to lay smoke to cover their withdrawal. At 1110 *Glasgow* was in the approach channel. Firing commenced shortly after noon, drawing a return fire that was heavy, persistent and accurate. The flashes from the batteries on shore could be clearly seen from the ship until smoke became too thick. To the accompaniment of loud crumps, fountains of white water erupted near the ship as *Glasgow* was straddled several times. Vernon was in the 4-inch ready room when the first straddle came over and recalls that it was more than a little disconcerting to hear the shrapnel banging on their thin armour. The 4-inch guns fired splash salvoes in an attempt to confuse the enemy spotters, to little avail; the Germans were taking the range from three shore-based radars. When the attack seemed especially heavy, the destroyers would bravely close with *Glasgow,* hoping to draw the fire away from her. Suddenly Vernon was aware of a crash and a shudder from somewheres aft, but in the excitement of action, with the noise of the ship's firing and the jarring vibrations from her departing salvoes, he did not realize it was a hit until white smoke, in stark contrast to the dark smoke from the 6-inch guns, billowed from *Glasgow's* port hangar area. She had received the first of two direct hits, which opened a large hole in the side and set a Carley float on fire. The burning float was quickly disposed of over the side by the Upper Deck Firefighting Party. The second hit was farther aft on the port side and did some damage to the galley and wardroom. No one was killed, but thirteen crew were wounded. *Glasgow* withdrew to assess damage, but breaking off was not to Captain Clarke's liking. Satisfied that the damage was not vital, he rejoined the action. Then, at 1330, the entire force withdrew for a space, while army personnel ashore assessed the effects of the bombardment. The signal from shore was, in effect, "Good shooting so far; carry on". Firing was resumed and again *Glasgow* was almost immediately straddled. Although the return fire was not now so hot, more straddles - one or two very close to the bridge -followed. Another signal from shore advised that advancing troops were now threatened by the "friendly fire" of the ships. The action was broken off and the whole force retired.

Desmond Tighe, Reuters correspondent, was on *Glasgow* during the action and filed the following story, headlined,

*"MIGHTY GUN DUEL; ALLIED SHIPS POUND CHERBOURG BATTERIES".*

*American battleships and heavy cruisers, supported by two British cruisers and a host of destroyers, fired broadside after broadside into German shore batteries at key points on the fringes of Cherbourg harbour. The bombardment started at eleven minutes past twelve and lasted for more than three hours, with German long range shore batteries returning the fire vigorously.*

*I watched this bombardment from the bridge of H.M.S. Glasgow, victor of the recent Bay of Biscay battle. She steamed steadily some 15,000 yards off the breakwater of Cherbourg Harbour as her six inch guns blazed away while the air resounded with the crash of broadside(s) from the other vessels.The Task Force, commanded by Rear-Admiral M. L. Deyo, U.S.N., flying his flag in the heavy cruiser Tuscaloosa, included the battleships Texas, Nevada, Arkansas, the American cruiser Quincy and the two British cruisers H.M.S. Glasgow and H.M.S.Enterprise, escorted by a strong force of American destroyers.*

*As we moved towards Cherbourg for the assault flotillas of minesweepers cleared the passage through mined areas. Overhead, silver against the blue sky, flew Lightnings, giving us constant fighter cover. It all seemed very peaceful as I watched a seagull flying in a leisurely manner in France.*

*All was calm on the bridge. Captain C.P.Clarke, D.S.O., sat on his little stool on the starboard side thoughtfully smoking his pipe. Just about noon we reached our bombardment zone with the little minesweepers still ahead. Quincy signalled "Proceed independently" and we broke from our battle line ahead.*

*I looked down on the pompom platforms and the 4-inch gun turrets to see men tightening their lifebelts and getting ready for action. On our port beam I could see through my glasses the outline of one of*

*the German forts.*

*Then the action began. The German shore batteries opened first at ten minutes past twelve sending over anti-personnel shells. Enterprise, lying on our starboard beam, started bombarding, flames and cordite curling from her 6-inch forward guns.*

*Nevada passed close to us and let fly a 14-inch broadside.*

*German shells were landing in groups of three just ahead of us. The minesweepers turned and we carried on to give them protection.*

*By now all ships were firing. Our forward turrets opened up and dazed by the roar I stuffed cotton wads in my ears. Destroyers and M.L.s were dropping smoke screens to cover us.*

*There were three ugly cracks as we were straddled close to our stern. The German gunnery was good. Nevada magnificently standing out of the smoke screen, the Stars and Stripes battle ensign flying at her topmast, turned away to starboard to take up another position and fired her after 14-inch guns with a roar. We were now being straddled by the shore batteries with alarming regularity and three shells landed just 15 yards ahead.*

*It was nearly 1 o'clock and some of the shore batteries had stopped but others carried on, and shrapnel tinkled on the bridge structure and on the side of the ship.*

*H.M.S.Enterprise was firing with all she had, and as she passed close to us the captain waved cheerfully from the bridge. Then things became really hot, for the batteries seemed to have got our range.*

*Admiral Deyo ordered retirement to the swept channel and for a time all was quiet. Twenty minutes later we were back again, firing at one stubborn battery to the southeast of Cherbourg. The others seemed to be out of action.*

*At a quarter to four, having been in action for three and a half hours, we steamed away, our mission ended.*

*The decks were littered with empty shell cases and shell splinters, and gun barrels were blackened with smoke. As we steamed towards our home port in the light of the setting sun men came up from the engine room, from the control posts far down in the bowels of the ship, from the cypher offices, men who had seen nothing of the action, but had just carried on doing their job, the while hearing the thumps of near misses, and the jar of the ship as broadsides were fired. But they were all elated. It had been a spirited action and H.M.S. Glasgow had added to her laurels.*[11]

The bombarding force reached Portland harbour about 1930. The main-brace was spliced in recognition of a job well done, and the ship's company got some rest. Admiral Deyo and the other captains gathered in Captain Clarke's cabin (rather more "ventilated" than it was before the action) to recap the day's work over a tot of rum.

Next day members of the ship's company were reading Desmond Tighe's dispatch and chuckling to themselves, for they hadn't seen the action in quite the heroic terms he used. They felt that, thanks to Tighe, they had stolen the show from the other ships. But as account succeeded account of the action, the men got a better sense of what they had accomplished. Historically, in duels between shore batteries and ships, the batteries win, especially when they are as numerous and as well protected as those at Cherbourg. Estimates that nineteen of the twenty-one forts had been silenced were probably exaggerated, but the fact remains that when the bombarding ships withdrew from Cherbourg, fire from the shore batteries had slackened very considerably and their threat to the ground forces was eliminated. They never fired landwards again, and when American infantry took the city they found the forts abandoned.

In Portland all on board had time to reflect on how lucky they had been. Only ten of their shipmates had to be transferred to hospital ashore. The hits were not on vital parts of the ship, although one old three badger whose kit was destroyed in the hangar took it rather personally: "They blew up me 'ome, they did, the bastards!", he complained to Vernon. The near misses were nearer and more dangerous than was first realized; closer examination in harbour revealed holes near the waterline, some of them three or four inches wide. and in the last analysis it was agreed that they owed much to the fact that the enemy had used high explosive shell with impact fuses. Had their shells been armour piercing, with delayed action fuses, the damage could have been considerable.

Young spirits tend not to dwell on what might have been; they are more apt to seize on the immediate. In this case, the immediate was Desmond Tighe's description of Captain Clarke calmly enjoying his pipe in the heat of battle. The shipwrights were engaged to fashion an oversize pipe, mounted on a stand, which the officers presented to the Captain in the wardroom as an affectionate and lighthearted recognition of his leadership.

As the bombardment fleet steamed away from Cherbourg, the Americans were tightening their grip on the city. By midnight units of the 79th Division had reached Fort du Roule, overlooking the dock area. On the 26th the tunnel sheltering von Schlieben's headquarters was attacked and the General taken prisoner. With him was the Naval Commander, Normandy, Rear Admiral Walther Hennecke, whose men had so thoroughly sabotaged and demolished the port facilities that it was weeks before the mess could be cleaned up and the docks used. By July 16, four Liberty ships unloaded in the harbour. By November, 14,000 tons of supplies were moving daily through the port. HMS *Glasgow*, and all in her, had helped make that happen; more than that, during and since D-Day the ship and her crew had done whatever was asked of them to assist the land forces in establishing and expanding their beachheads. As did all the participants in that great endeavour, they had risked everything, and they had been incredibly fortunate to have come through relatively unscathed. For survivors such as they, Shakespeare had written three and a half centuries earlier:

*He that outlives this day, and comes safe home,*
*Will stand a tip-toe when this day is nam'd,*[12]

For those whom Death found on June 6, 1944, and in the many days thereafter, there is an epitaph in the chapel of the Normandy American Cemetery and Memorial at Omaha Beach:

*"Think not only on their passing. Remember the glory of their spirit."*

In the Admiralty's laconic phraseology, HMS *Glasgow* had "sustained considerable though not major damage from shell hits"[13] in the action off Cherbourg on June 25, 1944. While that may well have been so, the consequence was that *Glasgow's* wartime service was ended. After receiving his new pipe, Captain Clarke announced that the ship was going to Newcastle for repair and refit. The crew would be paid off. At 1530 June 28, *Glasgow* left Portland, arriving at Plymouth five hours later. Deammunitioning done, the 1st Motor Boat and other previously discarded gear recovered, and farewells to old friends in the Plymouth Command having been made, *Glasgow* left the next day, turning north into the Bristol Channel and the Irish Sea, as she had done less than six weeks previously. The destroyers HMS *Undine, Urchin* and *Undaunted* were the escort; Vernon did not know it then, but he was to see much more of these three ships before war's end.

As on the last trip in these waters, Belfast Lough was *Glasgow's* destination. Then the Lough had been crammed with ships assembled for the great crusade to Normandy; now only a scattering of ships lay at anchor. Then they had stayed for more than a week of training and preparations; now they would pause in the Lough for a scant ten hours before continuing on around the north of Scotland and southwards to Newcastle-on-Tyne. For the Canadians on board the day had special significance: it was Dominion Day, July 1.

As at Plymouth, gear which had been put ashore when no one knew what fate awaited the ship and her people was collected back on board, and at 2200 *Glasgow* weighed and proceeded alone. A spirit of relief and relaxation pervaded the ship on this last voyage of her commission. Perils of shell and torpedo were past and long tense hours at the guns a memory. There would be time later for new assignments and fresh dangers; for the next few days it was enough to cruise peacefully in home waters, under normal ship's routine. Bill O'Neil describes the tenor of those days:

> [We were] sailing through the Outer Hebrides when suddenly the ship slowed and we dropped the Captain's Motor Boat over the side. It seems one of the R.N. boys lived on one of these islands,which only had ferry service once a week. So, the Captain's launch took him into his little island while we waited four miles offshore. I often wondered what he told his friends about this special service.
>
> ... we did a speed trial and even though the ship was going in for refit we hit 32 knots.[14]

Early the next day *Glasgow* docked at South Shields at the mouth of the

River Tyne. The morning was spent in removing the remaining ammunition to storage ashore, and in mid-afternoon the Captain spoke to his ship's company for the last time. The ship would be in refit for five months, he said, and everyone would get twenty-one days leave. Well, almost everyone would get leave. Not the Canadians: in bidding them farewell, the Captain said that they would return to *Niobe* to be redrafted into their own Navy. Within the week they had collected their kit, said their good-byes, and made the short journey to *Niobe* in Greenock. As for the ship herself, repair and refit would stretch beyond five months to twelve: by VE-Day, dockyard workers would have yet to finish with her.

For long afterwards, Vernon would reflect on his time in HMS *Glasgow* as the best of his naval experiences. She was what every sailor hoped for: a happy ship, commanded by good officers, crewed by good seamen and shipmates. With them he could proudly sing the ship's theme song, the old music hall piece, "I Belong To Glasgow":

> I belong tae Glesga, dear auld Glesga toon.
> But there's somethin' the matter wi' Glesga
> For it's gaein' roond and roond.
> I'm only a common auld workin' chap,
> As onyone here can see;
> But when I get a couple of drinks on a Sattiday
> Glesga belongs tae me!

To which, in reference to his ship, Vernon could add, "Aye, and that's richt!"

The Canadians were not long at *Niobe*. HMS *Sheffield*, a sister ship of *Glasgow*, had been lying in the Gareloch since the end of June. "Old Shiny", as she was affectionately known, had been detached from the Home Fleet at Scapa Flow after a long and hectic war during which she earned no fewer than twelve Battle Honours. No other ship of her class earned such laurels. Weary from more than 236,000 miles of steaming, but still proud, she was in dire need of refit to prepare her for the Pacific. British yards hadn't the space or the time for the job, so *Sheffield* was being sent off to Boston. Routine orders posted during the dog watches on July 17, 1944 gave the story:

Sailing Orders for Tuesday 18th July.
1030. Prepare for sea. Hoist 1st Motor Boat and Pulling C u t t e r s . A w a y 2nd Cutter with mail orderly.
1100. Mooring party of the Port Watch fall in in the Heads Flat. Harbour Close Range Weapons Crew up 2nd Motor Cutter.
1115. Special Sea Dutymen and Skeleton Damage Control Parties to your stations.
1200. Slip and proceed to sea.
1400.Starboard Watch to Defense Stations. Lookouts and Close  R a n g e Weapons' Crews of the White Watch close up.

1600. Action Stations.

1700. Secure. Assume Second State of Readiness. We shall remain at Second State of Readiness until 1200 noon Monday 24th July, securing again in South Boston Navy Yard, Boston, Massachusetts. U.S.A. The ship is to be prepared for operational service in the Pacific.

Sgd. G.M.Sladen, Commander.[15]

The fewer RN ratings sent to Boston for an extended "holiday" the better. The Canadians freshly come from *Glasgow* were drafted to *Sheffield* as temporary crew. Joining the ship on July 14, they were assigned regular watch-keeping duties for the passage to Boston.

An uneventful trip concluded in the Charles River at 0805 July 25. The crew was immediately put to work deamunnitioning ship. As they sweated in the hot Boston sun, they looked enviously at the truckloads of fresh provisions going to other ships in the dockyard. After months of the dried and salted rations of the RN, their mouths watered for a taste of this "real" food, but *Sheffield's* Supply Officer lacked either the will or the cash to buy anything until the last of his shipboard stores were consumed. It was too much for Vernon. With Joe LeClair, a Charlottetown lad serving in *Sheffield* whom he had met on board, he went that afternoon to the RCN Liaison Officer, begging an expedited passage to Halifax. Whether their request had any effect or not, all the Canadians were back in Halifax on July 29, where they were all given twenty-five days leave.

1. Comm. Colin Balfour RN, *Midshipman's Log.* Personal communication to Lawson Drake, September. 1999.

2. Lt. Cdr. R.C.C. McNab RN, *Letter to his Parents, June 14, 1944.* Original in Imperial War Museum, London. Copied to Lawson Drake, courtesy of IWM.

3. Winston Churchill, *The Second World War.* (London: Cassell & Co., Ltd 2nd ed, 1951) vol IV, 561.

4. J. Terraine, *Trafalgar.* (Ware, Herts.: Wordsworth Military ed, 1998) 135.

5. e.g.; Cornelius Ryan, *The Longest Day*; Stephen E. Ambrose, *D-Day, June 6,1944: The Climactic Battle of World War II.*

6. McNab, see 2 above.

7. Martin Blumenson, *Liberation.* (Alexandria, Va.: Time-Life Books Inc., 1978) 18.

8. McNab, see 2 above.

9. D. Botting, *The Second Front.* (Alexandria, Va.: Time-Life Books Inc., 1978)

10. Scot MacDonald, *Naval Guns At Cherbourg.* (Surface Warfare, May/June 1986) 24 - 27.

11. Desmond Tighe. Newspaper clipping, source unknown, copied to Lawson Drake by Bill O'Neil January 7, 1999.

12. *King Henry the Fifth, Act 4: Scene 3,*

13. *HMS Glasgow, Summary of Service.* (London: Imperial War Museum, Naval Historical Branch Pamphlet S 9515, 1979.)

14. Bill O'Neil to Lawson Drake, *Personal Communication,* January 7, 1999.

15. Ronald Bassett, *HMS Sheffield The Life and Times of Old Shiny.* (London: Arms and Armour Press, 1988.) 183

a).

b).

*Off Cherbourg, June 25, 1944. Pictures from HMS Enterprise.*
*a). Minesweepers clearing a lane towards shore.*
*b). The bombardment force. <u>Glasgow</u> dead ahead; to her port, in order: US destroyer; USS <u>Quincy;</u> US destroyer; USS <u>Nevada.</u>*
*IWM Neg. No. A24302 and A24301.*

a).

b).

c).

*HMS Glasgow off Cherbourg, June 25, 1944. Pictures from HMS Enterprise.*
*a). Glasgow emerging from smoke.*
*b). Straddled by shore batteries. Note shrapnel in the water and along Glasgow's starboard side.*
*c). Hit! Enemy shell strikes the port hangar area.*
*a & c: IWM Neg. No. A24304 and A24305*

a).

b).

*HMS <u>Glasgow:</u> the aftermath of battle.*
*a). Burial at sea.*
*b). Wounded being taken ashore. <u>Glasgow's</u> triple 6-inch "X" turret in the background.*

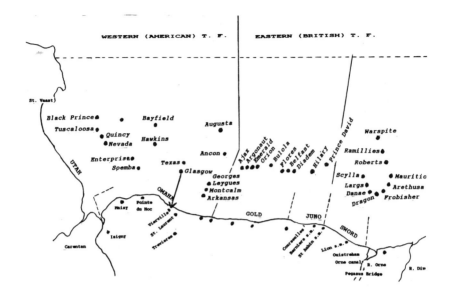

*Disposition of the heavy ships off the Normandy beaches on D-Day, June 6, 1944. The arrow indicates HMS Glasgow's first target area. (Modified from Tate, Costello and Hughes, D-Day.)*

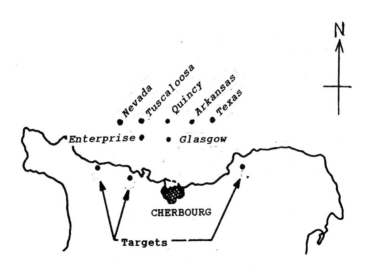

*Disposition of the heavy ships, bombardment of Cherbourg coastal forts, June 25, 1944. (Modified from MacDonald, Naval Guns at Cherbourg.)*

# 10. PREPARATION FOR THE PACIFIC: HMS UGANDA BECOMES HMCS UGANDA.

Vernon's leave in the summer of 1944 was quieter than previous ones. For one thing, travel was not as easy; wartime restrictions on gasoline and tires were being felt. For another, Vernon's experiences off Normandy in *Glasgow* had had a sobering effect on him. He had been under fire, his ship had been hit, and he had seen shipmates wounded. The quiet of home was a welcome change. He told us about some of the events in which he had participated. We read his copy of the inspirational message from the Commander-in-Chief, and we marvelled at the samples of "Action Rations" which he had brought home. These were rectangular tins, a little smaller than a cigarette packet, containing nourishment said to be equivalent to a complete meal. Each contained four dense cubes of enriched dehydrated food; two pieces of barley sugar candy; and two pieces of chewing gum. At least, they had contained chewing gum - in the two tins Vernon brought home, the seals had been broken and the pieces of gum (chiclets) removed.

Vernon was not to get to enjoy his full leave; in mid-August he was recalled to Halifax. At *Stadacona* he learned that he was being drafted to Canada's first World War II cruiser, "Ship S-343", then in the dockyard at Charleston, South Carolina. For the few days, while a draft was put together, he was placed in charge of a Shore Patrol whose task was to ensure good behaviour by naval personnel on the streets and in the public places of the city. He did not much relish his life as a naval policeman.

On August 29th his draft boarded the train in Halifax for a trip to Yarmouth. There they took the ferry to Bar Harbor, Maine, to catch another train south to Charleston, where they arrived on August 31. From his first glimpse of the ship, Vernon realized that there was a lot of work ahead, even if for the moment there would be a slack period until the workmen finished some of their tasks. Welders, mechanics, electricians, plumbers and who knew what other tradespeople swarmed over her, and gear lay all about her decks. Yet, through all the clutter and confusion, Vernon's practised eye recognized a swift cruiser, not unlike *Glasgow*, a little smaller, perhaps, but with the hull lines, superstructure and guns of her kind. Refloated, she would be a warship to carry the fight to the Japanese, for sure. But that was in the future; for the present it was enough to check into barracks ashore, to eat great American chow and to enjoy the weather.

The crew had been slowly gathering since early June. Each week, usually on Friday, additional drafts arrived. There would eventually be several Prince Edward Islanders in addition to Vernon in the ship's company. Some, such as Petty Officer Richard Curley and Able Seaman Joe LeClair, had had previous cruiser service, like Vernon, with the RN. Others, such as Leading Cook Frank Carragher, Acting Leading Seaman Lawson Tremere and Able Seaman Jack Thomson, had been in destroyers and/or corvettes. Some, such as Jim Grady, were joining their first ship. Vernon's journey from Halifax had been quite pleasant, but some of the others "enjoyed" trips that were riotous, bordering on the orgiastic. Vernon clearly remembers the stir caused by Jack Thomson's arrival. Jack describes the trip in his own words:

> *What a trip to Charleston! There was fellows on there I sailed with from other ships and from Boston on it was all party. There was a liquor store right in the station in Boston, and it's not too far from there to New York and another whack of liquor - I was in bad shape! We had our own private party in one of the smokers. Everybody knew each other, only one fellow I never knew , and we're drinking and this fellow I don't know, he was pouring the drinks. He didn't drink himself, and the s.o.b., he was pouring me rum, and vodka for a chaser, and after a while, you never noticed. He kept bugging me about P.E.I. and after three or four times I said, "Alright, that's enough; you've had your fun, now shut up". And he kept on, so I went to hit him and I went through that glass window in the smoker, and coming back I cut my hand all to hell - blood squirting to the ceiling. A Petty Officer took me back to the hospital car, but the doctor said he couldn't sew it up on the train. They were going to put me off in Washington, and I said, "If you put me off in Washington, that's the last you'll ever see of me in the Canadian Navy". I had seven charges against me when I got down there. I couldn't even feed myself. I guess the officer felt sorry for me, or something, and he said, "Thomson, we'll forget about these". I still have a piece of glass in my hand...[1]*

The antecedent of "Ship S 343" was a 6-inch cruiser laid down in John Brown's Yards on March 3, 1938. Launched on May 31, 1939 and completed May 17, 1940, she was the first in a class of 6-inch cruisers, more compact than previous ships and, by 1941, considered the best pattern for future building. She was christened HMS *Fiji*, and she gave her name to a class of eleven ships, all of which were named after British colonies. The *Fiji*-class cruisers were, in alphabetical order, HMS *Bermuda, Ceylon, Fiji, Gambia, Jamaica, Kenya, Mauritious, Newfoundland, Nigeria, Trinidad* and *Uganda* ("Ship S-343").

The careers of two of these ships were tragically short. *Fiji* survived a torpedo from *U-32* in September 1940, but it took six months to repair the damage. On May 22, 1941, barely two months after returning to service, she was bombed. Her forward engine and boiler rooms flooded rapidly, and in five hours she capsized and sank. HMS *Trinidad* was even more unlucky. On March 29, 1942, just five months after completion, she was hit by one of her own torpedoes which blew a hole forty-five feet by twenty feet in her port side and another one, ten feet by seven feet, in her starboard side. She was able to reach Kola Inlet and effect temporary repairs, but when she returned to sea she was bombed, a near miss blowing in the starboard patch. On May 5 1942 she was abandoned and scuttled.

Four other ships of the class suffered various misadventures but survived to war's end. *Kenya* took a torpedo far forward, *Newfoundland* took one on her rudder, and *Nigeria* one amidships near the foremast. *Uganda* escaped torpedoes only to fall victim to a radio-controlled bomb just eight months into her first commission.

HMS *Uganda* was laid down as Job J2509 on July 20, 1939 at the Vickers-Armstrong yard, North Shields, near Newcastle-on-Tyne. She was launched on August 7, 1941, commissioned on December 17, 1942 and completed on January 3, 1943. *Uganda* was 555 feet 6 inches long, with a beam of sixty-two feet. She had a draught of twenty feet forward and twenty feet eight inches aft. She displaced 8,800 tons. With four Parsons shaft-geared turbines drawing steam from Admiralty 3-drum boilers producing 72,500 shaft horsepower, she had a top speed of 31.5 knots. Most ships of the class mounted twelve 6-inch guns in four triple turrets, but *Uganda* (and *Ceylon* and *Newfoundland*) had only nine - in two turrets forward and one aft. Her secondary armament comprised eight 4-inch HA/LA quick-firing guns in double mounts, two 2-pounders, eight 40mm pom-poms in two quadruple mounts, a number of Oerlikons(20mm cannon) and six 21-inch torpedo tubes. In addition, these ships were equipped to carry two Walrus aircraft in hangars on each side.

After initial workups out of Newcastle, *Uganda* went north to Scapa Flow, where she remained during January and February of 1943. Early in March she departed Scapa, sailing down the west coast of Britain to Plymouth. After a short stay in Drake's home port, she left for Freetown, Sierra Leone, reaching there on March 24. Her stay was brief; she was soon prowling the ocean in search of a blockade runner expected from the Far East. In spite of having launched her Walrus aircraft to extend the range of her search, the blockade runner was not intercepted.

In May 1943 the tedium of patrolling was relieved by an interesting change of duty: escorting Cunard's *Queen Mary* carrying Winston Churchill across the Atlantic to a conference in Washington. Keeping station one mile to starboard of the "*Q. M.*" at thirty knots for five days was a strenuous test of *Uganda's* machinery, and of the nerves of her crew. A brief interlude of routine followed this work-out, but by the middle of June *Uganda* was en route to the Mediterranean, where Malta became her home base. Malta was still subject to air attack at this time, and the A.A. guns on *Uganda* were kept busy. The ship's real role, however, was to be part of Force K in support of Allied landings in Sicily. She left Malta on July 9, 1943 to take up her position off the Sicilian coast at H-hour, 0245 July 10. She went close inshore with the assaulting forces, giving supporting fire during the landings and securing the flanks against counter-attack. In the days that followed she engaged shore batteries north of Syracuse, rescued survivors from the hospital ship *Talamba* and continued bombarding, striking Augusta on the 11th and Melilli on the 12th. Enemy retaliation was mostly in the form of air attacks, and there were several near misses from bombs. At the end of July HMS *Newfoundland* was torpedoed in the stern by an Italian submarine. The cruiser survived, and later would serve with *Uganda* in the Pacific; the submarine was sunk.

The battle for Sicily lasted forty days. The next objective was the Italian mainland and the first landings, across the Strait of Messina, occurred on September 3. Six days later, in Operation Avalanche, the U.S. Fifth Army landed at Salerno. *Uganda* provided supporting fire, directed by forward observers ashore who pinpointed gun positions, tank concentrations, ammunition dumps, road junctions and bridges. From a firing position about a mile and a half off shore the ship was essentially a stationary artillery battery; as such, she was a tempting target for enemy bombers.

At this time the Germans were using a radio-controlled bomb, the PC 1400X, or Fritz-X, known to our forces as "Chase-me-Charlie". Released from its carrier plane at 32,500 feet, the one and three-quarter ton armour-piercing bomb, with its 700 pounds of explosive, fell at a speed of nearly 750 mph. On September 12, *Uganda* had a near miss from a Fritz-X, but on the 13th, at 1448, her luck ran out. A Fritz-X, fired from a Dornier 217K-2, hit the HA/LA director, passed through seven decks, including the armour plate over the after engine room, and exited through the ship's bottom to explode in the water beneath the hull. Seventeen crewmen were killed and seven wounded; both after engines were put out; the outer starboard shaft was so bent that its engine had to be shut down; and severe structural damage was accompanied by considerable flooding.

Prompt and efficient damage control saved the ship. She limped back to Malta on her one remaining engine (the port forward), made temporary repairs, then proceeded to Gibraltar for drydocking. With properly welded patches sealing her hull, and with her three useless propellers removed and stowed on board, she left Gibraltar on November 7, 1943 in convoy for Charleston, where she arrived at the end of the month. She had been in commission just eight months since her completion.[2]

That is how HMS *Uganda* became "Ship S 343" in the Charleston Navy Yard where, throughout the summer of 1944, her Canadian crew was assembling. When the full complement was gathered they would number just over 900, of whom about one third - officers and ratings - had served in cruisers of the Royal Navy. Seven percent of the ship's company would be RCN. The average age of the crew would be 23.6 years. The youngest rating was seventeen years old; 130 were aged twenty. Just over twenty-eight percent would be married men.

On her arrival at Charleston, *Uganda's* ammunition had been removed to storage in bunkers ashore. A large rectangular hole had been cut in her decks above the after engine and boiler rooms. The damaged engines, boilers, shafts, broken and weakened bulkheads, shoring timbers, debris and other damaged structures were removed through this hole. The rent in her bottom was properly replated, and the dark, smelly fuel oil which covered all surfaces where flooding had occurred was cleaned up. When replacement boilers, turbines, and shafts arrived from the U.K. they were lowered into position through the hole, after which bulkheads and decks were welded back into place. The three enormous propellers were reattached to their shafts, and various tradespeople restored the many services that would eventually bring life back to the ship.

The assembling Canadian sailors were no mere spectators of their future ship's rebirth. The use of cutting or welding torches always presented a fire hazard, especially where oil was present, and many ratings stood fire watch with extinguishers when such work was in progress. There was old paint to be removed and fresh paint to be applied inside the ship and out. Every day Vernon oversaw a work party in some part of the ship. The ammunition in storage had to be cleaned and inspected; many gunnery ratings, including Jim Grady, spent their days at this task. Cleaning the shells, inspecting fuses and labelling suspect material for demolition was dangerous work, but at least it was cool in the bunkers at the ammunition depot. Jim Grady recalls how he and his mates were required to wear fresh white coveralls at work, and how they moved about the large depot on motor scooters over roads on which hundreds of snakes basked in the heat.[3]

As work in one section of the ship was completed, that area had to cleared of loose gear and restored to proper naval order. Naval order was being restored, too, to the heretofore somewhat relaxed discipline of life in the repair yards. "Rig of the Day" became obligatory, and "Divisions" a regular routine, as the ship's company was eased back into the formalities of the Service.

After ten months of repair in drydock "S 343" returned to her element. Basin trials early in October preceded her first voyage on the Cooper River. Painting, provisioning, fuelling and ammunitioning filled the days until commissioning day, October 21, 1944. On the 139th anniversary of Trafalgar, Nelson's last victory. "S 343" was commissioned HMCS *Uganda*. The Commanding Officer was Captain Rollo Mainguy RCN; his Executive Officer was Commander H.F. Pullen, RCN.

Retention of *Uganda's* original name was a departure from RCN custom, which was to rename ships which had previously been commissioned in the Royal Navy. The British Colonial Office had made special representations to Canadian Naval Headquarters to retain the name, citing the British-ruled East African Protectorate's special interest in the ship that bore its name. Uganda (the Protectorate) had contributed to the purchase of HMS *Uganda's* aircraft and had presented the ship with ceremonial silk flags and six silver bugles. So, by a decision at a high level, the name was retained. The ship's crest was also kept, with a slight modification: three maple leaves were added to the top of the shield, above the crowned crane.

Old sailors have numerous superstitions about ship's names. Most agree that a name change brings a change in a ship's fortune; the argument is as to whether the change is for the better or worse. As events would later show, it was *Uganda's* good fortune never to suffer further damage from the enemy; it would be her bad fortune, and the bad fortune of her crew, to end her wartime service in a manner unlike that of any other warship. And, after that, her name was changed.

1.  Jack Thomson, recorded conversation, March 20, 2000.

2.  Stephen C. Geneja, *The Cruiser Uganda. One War - Many Conflicts.* (Corbyville, Ont.: Tyendinaga Publishers, 1994) Ch1 The definitive history of HMS/HMCS *Uganda.* Interested readers should consult this book for detail.

3.  James Grady, Recorded conversation January 6, 1998.

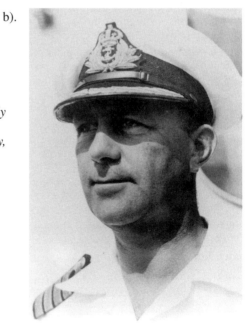

a). HMCS _Uganda_ immediately
after repair and refit, Charleston.
b). Captain E. Rollo Mainguy,
_Uganda's_ Comomanding Officer.

## 11. HMCS UGANDA: WORKING UP A CANADIAN CRUISER.

The ship's company hosted a commissioning dance ashore on the night of October 23. It was a way to celebrate their ship's rebirth and to say thanks to the Americans who had treated them so kindly. At 0909 next morning HMCS *Uganda* cast off from Pier "A", Charleston Navy Yard, for the last time, bound for Halifax. The long voyage to the Pacific had begun.

That first day at sea a couple of small fires, the last legacy of the long refit, had to be extinguished but in general an uneventful passage brought *Uganda* to the gate at Halifax on October 25. Slowly she passed George's Island and drew up to a Dockyard pier. During five days in port, additional stores were loaded, and on the 30th of the month, without fanfare, Canada's first World War II cruiser slipped for the open Atlantic. For Vernon and other "big ship" sailors this voyage was nothing new, but for the boys from the corvette navy, it was a novel experience! The ship's motion was so much easier, and the mess decks remained dry; above all, there was no convoy to shepherd. *Uganda* steamed alone, and at her own speed; the electrical circuits to her guns needed more work before she would be in fighting condition, and she did not want to encounter anyone during the crossing.

*Uganda* was returning to familiar haunts - Scapa Flow and Newcastle. On November 4 she threaded her way into the bleak anchorage at Scapa to fuel and spend the night. Next morning she left for Newcastle, arriving on November 6 for a five-week's stay in yard and drydock. The crew was rotated off on seven-day leaves, to London or Edinburgh for sightseeing, or perhaps to visit relatives. It was at Newcastle that a problem that was to be a consistent defect of life on board first came to a head: food quality. Not very good on the trip across the Atlantic, the food became so bad in port that one day there was a mass refusal to eat. Officers investigating this serious breach of discipline found it justified. (Indeed, their own food was no better.) Nobody was punished, and attempts were made to improve food quality, but complaints of poor messing (justifiable or not) remained a fact of life in *Uganda*.

When questioned about food quality, Vernon finds the complaints hard to defend, claiming he never went hungry. There was poor quality meat from time to time and later, on operations, everyone would become thoroughly sick of dehydrated vegetables and eggs. Victualling was done by the Royal Navy, leading Vernon to suppose that his time in HMS *Glasgow* accustomed him to plain fare, whereas ratings direct from RCN found quite a difference in food. Frank Carragher, a Leading Cook, remembers that good quality provisions were taken on board. He baked fresh bread daily, and made biscuits, but he,too, deplored the quality of dried foods.

On December 12 the ship left Newcastle for Rosyth, passing under the Forth Bridge to reach the dockyard on the 13th. Some crew took the Liberty Boat across the river to South Queensferry and a bus to Edinburgh seven miles away. Like millions of tourists before and since, they viewed the castle, strolled along

Princes Street and the Royal Mile, and warmed to the Scots hospitality of "Auld Reekie".

The next day *Uganda* returned to Scapa Flow, entering the deep water, almost landlocked, basin through a passage not guarded by mines nor blocked by sunken ships. Scapa was the base for the British Home Fleet, and the graveyard of the World War I German High Seas Fleet, interned there and scuttled on June 21, 1919. The base was considered impregnable until the night of October 13/14, 1939, when Lieutenant Gunther Prien, in *U-47*, penetrated its defenses and torpedoed the battleship *Royal Oak* at her mooring, with the loss of 786 of her crew.

Scapa Flow was a grey cheerlessness place, described by Bob Cross as "a place no one should want"[1]. The daylight hours were few in this latitude at this time of year and the sun rarely emerged from the low clouds. Apart from a NAAFI* canteen, there were few amenities ashore. Vernon was not impressed, and was glad to be kept busy, for with her return to Scapa, *Uganda's* working up began in earnest. There were firefighting and damage control courses ashore, torpedo firing (with dummy warheads) and recovery at sea. As coxswain of one of the motor boats Vernon had the job of retrieving the spent torpedoes. In the anchorage, when his boat was Duty Boat, he ran errands among ships and between ship and shore.

The shortening December days were leading up to Vernon's fifth Christmas away from home. On December 23, HMCS *Sioux*, back from escorting a convoy to Russia, came alongside to add an additional Canadian presence to the festive day. The 25th was marked by Captain's rounds at 1100, followed by turkey dinner. Two long established Naval traditions were observed: the mainbrace was spliced (an extra issue of rum for the day); and the youngest member of the crew wore the Captain's four gold stripes and "commanded" the ship for part of the day. Dinner and traditions notwithstanding, hearts and thoughts turned to homes and loved ones so recently left, and with whom reunions could well be a long way into the future. Vernon certainly felt the nostalgia of the day.

On the last day of the year, in characteristic misty weather, *Uganda* sailed from Scapa accompanied by an escort carrier. During the afternoon the crew watched the carrier's Swordfish aircraft practising takeoffs and landings. How many on board realized that what they were seeing for the first time would become routine in the operational days ahead, although with more modern aircraft than the venerable "Stringbags"?

Overnight *Uganda* rounded the north of Scotland, and steamed south to enter the Clyde, passing up the wide firth to an anchoring buoy at Greenock. From the dockyard there spare parts for British submarines in Fremantle, Australia, were embarked and stowed near one of the hangars. By 2100 the ship was under way again, bound for Gibraltar.

*Uganda* steamed in waters more friendly for Allied shipping than they had been a year earlier when *Glasgow* and *Enterprise* challenged German destroyers' right to sea room. Nevertheless, gun crews closed up at dawn and dusk, just in

---

* Navy, Army, Air Force Institute. A catering service to the British Armed Forces.

case of a lurking enemy. Biscay lived up to its stormy reputation as, on the second day out, *Uganda* was rolling through wet and windy weather. By noon on the 5th the ship was in Gibraltar. A few fortunate libertymen, including Vernon, were piped ashore for the afternoon while the ship refuelled. As far as Vernon was concerned, nothing at "Gib" had changed since his firat visit some eleven months previously.

At 2000, *Uganda* returned to sea. Shortly after leaving Gibraltar, with Oran somewhere off to starboard, she passed the spot where on February 6, 1943, the corvette HMCS *Louisburg,* Frank Carragher's last ship, had been sunk by Italian aircraft. Frank had been thrown overboard, then sucked under water by the plunging vessel, only to be blown to the surface when armed depth charges exploded. Others in the water were seriously injured in the explosion, but he was only mildly concussed.[2] Thirty-eight of his shipmates were lost.

Now the Mediterranean was not the hostile sea that he and *Uganda* had earlier known. The Italian Air Force no longer existed, and there were no more Dorniers with their Fritz-X's. *Uganda's* A.A. crews were not closed up after leaving Gibraltar. Pantellaria was passed at 0820 on the 7th, and by 1500 the ship was entering Valetta harbour, to secure, with some difficulty, to a buoy. Looking over the anchorage, Vernon could see the upper works and masts of ships sunk by enemy aircraft during the long aerial siege of the "George Cross Island", and not yet salvaged.

The stop in Malta was for just over twenty-four hours. There was time for leave to explore Valetta's narrow streets and to take on board a draft of RN personnel as passengers to Alexandria. Maltese souvenir salesmen, with lace and other articles, were on board in the morning before sailing, but the sailors found their prices very expensive. Most of them, like Vernon, could not afford more than a small piece of lace work for mother, wife or girl friend at home.

*Uganda* departed Malta late in the afternoon of January 8, bound for Alexandria. During the trip, the crew attended sick bay for inoculations against tropical diseases, and for a day or so there were sore arms from the needles. Their sister ship HMS *Newfoundland,* Pacific-bound like themselves, was sighted, and for some of January 9, at least, the African coast was visible off to starboard. On the 10th, nearing Alexandria, the A.A. gunners practised against friendly aircraft. In the early afternoon the ship entered Alexandria harbour.

The course into harbour passed near Aboukir Bay, the location of the Battle of the Nile. Thus, since leaving Britain, *Uganda* had passed the vicinities of three of Nelson's great victories: Cape St. Vincent, The Nile and Trafalgar. Whether *Uganda's* people were aware of this or, if they were, whether it mattered to them, is unknown. But they were to be in Alexandria for the next five weeks to acquire, through workups, something of the "Nelson spirit" to take with them to the war in the Pacific.

Later in the day, when he had a few moments to survey the harbour, Vernon spied an old acquaintance from earlier days: moored to a buoy not far from *Uganda's* anchorage was HMCS *Prince Henry*. She had just delivered 247 New Zealand troops from Europe on the first leg of their return trip home, and was in harbour awaiting orders. Although Vernon could not know it, her commander was Capt. V. S. Godfrey, his last skipper in HMCS *Prince David.* Later, during their stay in "Alex", Capt. Mainguy would entertain Capt. Godfrey, with the captains of HMS *Arethusa* and *Nubian,* to dinner, but Vernon does not remember Capt. Godfrey leaving *Uganda's* wardroom to look up his old fishing buddy from west coast Canadian days!

As for *Prince Henry,* she was never to see Canada again. During a refit at the East India Docks in London, she was paid off in April, 1945. The RN used her for a short time before she was sold in 1946 to the Ministry of Wartime Transport. Renamed *Empire Parkeston,* she ferried troops between the Hook of Holland and Harwich. She ended her days in a breaker's yard in La Spezia, Italy in 1962.[3]

The first priority after securing in harbour was cleaning and painting to undo the ravages of the long trip from Charleston. Work parties on deck and over the side chipped away rust, applied paint and generally spruced up their ship. The crew was spared one of the nastiest cleaning jobs: scouring the bilges of their foul and greasy water. Local boys, ten to twelve years of age, were hired for this loathsome task. Such a practice would now be frowned upon, but the boys fitted well into the confined spaces of the bilges and they appreciated the money.

Even in January, and on the Mediterranean coast, the Egyptian days could be hot. A new ship's routine was introduced. Working parties fell in at 0600 and worked until breakfast at 0700. Although the effect of the change was to get more work done in the coolest part of the day, the new routine was not popular with many of the hands, who resented having to turn out an hour earlier in the morning.

On the 12th they went to sea for the day for degaussing tests.* On Monday, the 14th, workups began in earnest, as *Uganda* and *Newfoundland* went to sea together to exercise their 6-inch gun crews. One ship towed a target barge at a calculated safe distance astern while the other ship fired on it and an aircraft spotted the fall of shot. After a certain number of rounds the roles of towing ship and shooting ship were reversed. All aspects of gunnery were exercised: ranging, corrections, salvos, rapidity of fire, etc. Nor were the 4-inch HA and pom-pom crews idle: they practised on drogues towed by an aircraft. On occasion, the pom-pom crews drilled on a range ashore while the crews of the heavier guns exercised at sea. An intense rivalry developed between the "Kips" in *Newfoundland* and the Canucks in *Uganda,* with each side claiming the better gunnery. Whatever the validity of these claims, the competition and the constant drill had the desired effect of increasing the efficiency and the effectiveness of shooting on both ships.

Torpedo firing practice was not neglected, either. As a Scapa, Vernon was coxswain of the ship's boat detailed to recover the spent torpedoes and return them to the ship. On one such mission, he neglected to keep well clear of the ship's stern when approaching the after boom; instead he "cut the corner" by

---

* Steel ships radiate a magnetic field which will detonate magnetic mines. Degaussing is the neutralization of a ship's magnetic field by electrially charged cables encircling the hull.

passing too close. Just as he was rounding the stern. *Uganda's* engines gave a kick, and Vernon was very lucky that his boat safely cleared the propeller wash. His error did not pass unnoticed, and he was duly reprimanded for his lapse in seamanship.

Workups included night exercises, too. In company with the Italian destroyer *Artigliore* (on the Allied side since the Italian surrender) the ship's company was drilled in station keeping, starshell illumination and night gunnery.

Despite the intensity of the training, time was found for leisure - leisure, that is, after due observance of naval etiquette. Sunday mornings in harbour began with the full pomp of Sunday Divisions, including colour guard and band. All the ship's company not actually on watch, or in possession of some other valid excuse, mustered on deck in their best uniforms, later to be dismissed to their messes for Captain's rounds. Church services followed, Protestant and Roman Catholic in separate locations, with shore leave in the afternoon. For those who could not get ashore, entertainment came on board; one afternoon an Egyptian magician performed for an attentively sceptical audience in the port hangar.

Going ashore in Alexandria was for Vernon and most of the young Canadians their first introduction to an ancient culture and to Islam. It was also their first exposure to a level of poverty they could not have imagined. Their earliest culture shocks came when they saw local people rummaging in their ship's garbage for bits of food, clothing and any salvageable item of potential use. On one occasion, Vernon was moved to ask Frank Carragher for some food from the ship's stores to give to the starving scavengers. Frank found a large tin of processed meat - "Spam" - which no one was likely to miss but when the recipients of this generosity discovered its pork content, it was of no further value to them. Some of them felt very insulted by this unwitting affront to their religious customs, and would have vented their rage on their naive benefactors, could they have gotten on board.

The social and economic life of the bazaars were new experiences, too. The sailors learned to drink the strong Turkish coffee in the sidewalk cafes and, above all, they learned the fine art of haggling. Whether they realized that hard bargaining was taken for granted in the local economy, or whether they felt compelled to haggle because of their own shortage of money is immaterial. No one ever paid the first, or even the second asking price as they sought gifts for loved ones at home. After a round of hard bargaining, Vernon bought a camel leather lady's purse, garishly decorated with representations of the Pyramids. (When he got home he gave it to his mother, but she never could bring herself to use it. It remains unused to this day, an enduring souvenir of a boy's love, if not a tribute to his taste!)

With longer leaves than an afternoon pass it was possible to make the 100-mile trip to Cairo, and beyond to Giza, to see the Pyramids and the Sphinx. Vernon went with a group led by one of the chaplains. Besides viewing the ancient monuments, he rode a camel and like many of his mates had his picture printed over postcard scenes of the Nile and even on a facsimile of an Egyptian bank note.

Evening leaves were also granted in Alexandria. For those who tired of the coffee shops and the bazaars, the RN-managed Fleet Club offered a decent meal and a pot of beer, showers with unlimited water and haggle-free shopping. All ratings under the age of twenty, however, were required to back on board by 2245!

On board, in addition to the usual shipboard routine, ammunition parties were busy loading shells and charges for use in training shoots at sea. Shore bombarding exercises were carried out off Ra's al Kana'is, a sharp cape jutting into the Mediterranean about 150 miles west of Alexandria. It is not far from El Alamein, and shore parties from the ship visited two graveyards there; one was the cemetery for casualties of the battles of October, 1942; the other "graveyard" was a huge parking area jammed with masses of German armour and other equipment taken during the campaign.

It was now February. The heat had increased noticeably and was felt all the more acutely when the ship returned from "outside". It would soon be time to leave "Alex", and few would be sorry. Before her departure, *Uganda* was reminded of her earlier service in the Mediterranean when, on February 11th, her wardroom was host to officers from USS *Savannah* which had been Fritz-bombed at Salerno on September 11th , 1943.

The next day *Uganda* went to sea with Vice Admiral Tennant on board, for a final exercise on the firing range. Having earned the Vice Admiral's approval of her performance, *Uganda* slipped and proceeded to sea on February 13th, at 1802, after thirty-three days of the most intensive training by any Canadian warship. Three hours out, Rosetta, which lies at the mouth of the western branch of the Nile, was passed to starboard; early next morning the light on Ra's al Barr, marking the eastern mouth of the river, was sighted on the same beam. Ahead lay Port Said and the Suez Canal. The Canal pilot came on board at 0430, inside the Said breakwater. At 0529 he took *Uganda* into the Canal at a smart 13 knots.

The Suez Canal is essentially a ditch, 105 miles long, cut North to South across the Isthmus of Suez, connecting Port Said in the north to Suez in the south. There are no locks because the Mediterranean Sea and the Red Sea are at the same level and the terrain across the isthmus is flat. When the Canal opened on November 17, 1869, the sea route from England to India was shortened by thousands of miles. Initially the Canal was twenty-six feet deep, 230 feet wide at the surface and seventy-two feet at the bottom. With successive enlargements to accommodate ever larger vessels, the canal is now forty-six feet deep, almost 400 feet wide at the surface, and 118 feet wide at the bottom. Dredges work continuously to prevent infilling by blowing sand.

The Canal from Port Said enters Lake Timsah: the cut continues through Timsah and into Great Bitter Lake. Near here southbound ships wait in the Al Ballah bypass until northbound traffic passes. The Suez pilot left *Uganda* while she lay in the bypass: Commander Pullen made good use of the waiting time by allowing hands to swim off the port side in water at sixty-three degrees Fahrenheit.

1. Robert Cross, *Personal Diary*.
   Able Seaman Bob Cross kept a small diary, in which he made daily entries during almost the entire cruise of *Uganda*, but when he left the ship in Esquimalt he left his diary behimd. A shipmate found it on top of a locker, but it had no name attached, only the initials R. G. C.. The finder of the diary took it to reunions of *Uganda's* crew until ultimately its author was identified. Several copies of the diary were made;  Kay Horgan and Vernon Drake lent me their copies.

2. Frank Carragher, recorded coversation, April 22, 2000.

3. Ken MacPherson and John Burgess, *The Ships of Canada's Naval Forces 1910 - 1981* (Toronto: Collins, 1981)

*Working up. A practice salvo from "A" and "B" turrets, off Ra's al Kana'is, Egypt. View fro HMCA <u>Uganda's</u> bridge.*

a).

b).

a). *Barren Aden.*
*Windmills at a salt*
*works.*
b). *The Suez*
*Canal.*
*(Diagrammatic,*
*not to scale).*

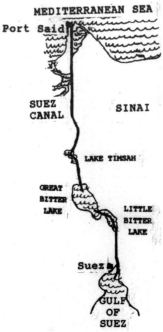

## 12. WHITE ENSIGN vs RISING SUN:
## THE ROYAL NAVY IN THE PACIFIC, 1941 - 1944.


Let us leave Vernon and *Uganda*, for a little space, in the warm waters of the Suez Canal bypass while we review the Royal Bavy's actions against Japan after the attack on Pearl Harbor.

The naval war in the Pacific was all in Japan's favour at the beginning. The element of surprise (or treachery, as some would call it) at Pearl Harbor; the brave and skilful execution of shrewd tactics in subsequent engagements; the deployment of the finest equipment against ill-equipped, unprepared adversaries; and the relentless pursuit of a clearly defined objective gave the Japanese Imperial Navy, for a time, total command of Pacific waters.

Aggression over land and across the waters in December 1941 and through the early months of 1942 established Japanese territorial dominance over a wide arc extending almost two thousand miles beyond the Home Islands. It would not be until the Battles of the Coral Sea and Midway in the first and last weeks of May, 1942, respectively, that the Japanese tide of victory would be checked by the United States Navy. From that time forward to war's end, the Pacific Ocean was American water.

Almost as a side effect to Japanese Imperial aggression, a British naval presence in the Pacific theatre was practically wiped out. Readers desiring a detailed account of the Royal Navy's near eclipse and subsequent re-emergence in the Pacific would be well advised to read Edwyn Gray's book, *Operation Pacific*.[1]

The sorry chronicle of British Empire naval losses to the Imperial Japanese Navy begins with the tragedy of Force Z. This small fleet, commanded by Admiral Tom Phillips and comprising the new battleship HMS *Prince of Wales*, the battle cruiser HMS *Repulse*, and the destroyers HMS *Express, Electra, Tenedos* and HMAS *Vampire*, left Singapore December 8, 1941, to attack a Japanese invasion fleet off northern Malaya. Two days later, in an action lasting barely ninety minutes, Japanese bombers sank the two battleships, effectively destroying Force Z.

In depressingly rapid succession, the torpedo boats, gunboats, destroyers and cruisers comprising the remnant of British naval forces in Pacific waters were destroyed by Japanese surface and/or aerial forces. Then a new Eastern Fleet - a mixed armada of four obsolete battleships, three aircraft carriers (one old, slow and small, the others new but not yet worked up), two heavy cruisers, four light cruisers and thirteen destroyers - was assembled in the Indian Ocean. In two encounters with the Japanese early in April, this fleet was soundly defeated, with the loss of several ships. Vice-Admiral Sir James Somerville was ordered to withdraw the surviving ships to Kilindini on the east African coast.

Just as it had been swept from the Pacific, the Royal Navy was now driven from the Indian Ocean. But there was a major difference: the fleet which

Somerville took to Kilindini remained a potent force, especially if it could be augmented with appropriate air support.

Unknown to anyone then, there would be no more Royal Navy defeats in the Indian Ocean or the Pacific. Grievous losses there would be, but no more humiliations of the scale of the first five months of the Pacific war. The winds sown by the Japanese strike forces would soon ripen into whirlwinds for their reaping. The first of the harvest would be at the Coral Sea, May 4 - 8, the first battle in naval history between two fleets which never saw each other[2]. In terms of the battle itself, it was the barest of Allied victories, but its far larger result was to turn back an invasion force from Port Moresby, and to stop Japan's advance southwards for the first time since Pearl Harbor.

Japanese Admiral Isoroku Yamamoto had one more hand to play: by invading Midway Atoll he hoped to lure the remainder of the American Pacific Fleet, especially its carriers which had escaped Pearl Harbor, to their destruction. (Part of his plan was a diversionary attack on the Aleutians, details of which have already been described.) Yamamoto commanded a force of eighty-six warships, including eleven capital ships and six carriers. Opposing him were Rear-Admiral Raymond Spruance USN and Rear-Admiral Frank Fletcher USN with twenty-eight ships - three carriers screened by nothing larger than 8-inch cruisers - in two Task Forces. The Japanese had 304 aircraft, the Americans 233.

The battle began after first light on the morning of June 4 with a Japanese raid by 108 planes on Midway. As the surviving aircraft from this raid were rearming and refuelling aboard their carriers, dive-bombers from the USS *Enterprise* and *Yorktown* screamed down, so crippling the *Akagi, Kaga* and *Soryu* in a six-minute attack that they all sank within a few hours. The Japanese struck back with a forty-plane attack from the remaining large Japanese carrier, the *Hiryu*, against the *Yorktown*. The American flat-top, the beloved "Waltzing Matilda", hit with three bombs and four torpedoes, was heavily, but not mortally damaged*. Late in the afternoon planes from the *Enterprise* found the *Hiryu*, and reduced her to sinking condition as well. The enemy carrier strike force that had been the scourge of the Pacific was thus obliterated.

While the battle of Midway was America's first great naval victory of the war, it did not end U.S. Navy defeats. Two months later, at the Battle of Savo Island, for example, with superior gunnery and well executed night-action tactics, the Japanese won a major victory over a confused and ineptly led American fleet. (The Australian 8-inch cruiser HMAS *Canberra* was lost in this action.) Only in retrospect was the true significance of Midway understood: with the tactical heart of its Navy removed, Japan's aggressive expansion was ended. At Midway, the United States had bought time: time to build more capital ships; time to complete and equip a new generation of large carriers; time to deploy these carriers with accompanying capital ships and support ships as Fleets and Task Forces which would eventually carry punishing naval air power right up to the Home Islands of Japan.

---

\* She was taken under tow, and twenty-four hours later was twice torpedoed by *I-168*. She sank in two thousand fathoms June 7, 1942.

The Royal Navy borrowed that time to regroup, reorganize, reinforce and prepare for a return to action against Japan, utilizing all the aircraft carriers that it could muster. Two years after its ignominious withdrawal, a rejuvenated Eastern Fleet was back in the Pacific, attacking Japanese installations in the East Indies. Its final action was against Nicobar Island on October 17, 1944. Five weeks later it was divided into two: the East Indies Fleet and the British Pacific Fleet (BPF).

As early as the summer of 1944, Prime Minister Churchill was pressing President Roosevelt to authorize an expanded role for a British Pacific Fleet, but Admiral Ernest King, the U.S. Chief of Naval Operations, did not want (and really did not need) the Royal Navy in his theatre. King nursed a deep antipathy towards the British, alleged to have been rooted in the debacle of convoy PQ-17. In July of 1942 this Russia-bound convoy was abandoned by its Royal Navy escorts on orders from the Admiralty, which believed that heavy German surface units were at sea. The convoy was subsequently decimated by U-boats and the Luftwaffe. It is said that, based on this event, King distrusted Royal Navy staff work and questioned the resolution of its admirals in action.

Admiral Sir Bruce Fraser (to whom command of the Eastern Fleet had passed in August 1944, and who assumed command of the British Pacific Fleet) was also eager  to ensure a Royal Navy contribution to the defeat of Japan, in spite of King's deep-rooted conviction that the war could be quite successfully prosecuted without the British. Fraser lobbied Admiral Nimitz, and later General MacArthur, to have the BPF attached to Nimitz's command in the central Pacific, until King was forced to make some arrangement. The most that King would concede was to establish the BPF as a task force of the U.S. Fifth Fleet. Fraser accepted and with his acceptance agreed to his own reduced status from fleet commander to task force commander.

British participation would require adoption of the American system of signalling, and the use of the U.S. Navy base at Manus, in the Admiralty Islands. Although the Admiralty Islands were British, Manus was controlled by the Americans. The RN officially was to have access only to the anchorage and the bulk fuel stores. Unofficially, however (that is, without Admiral King's knowledge) the generous Yanks made available every resource the Brits required.

While the administrative details of combining the fleets were being worked out, HM ships were in action, gaining experience in the art and practice of Fleet Air assaults. HMS *Illustrious, Indomitable, Newcastle, Black Prince, Argonaut, Kempenfelt, Wessex, Whirlwind, Wakeful* and *Wrangler* left Trincomalee on December 17, 1944 under command of Rear-Admiral Sir Philip Vian to carry out two strikes against targets on Sumatra. On January 16, 1945, an even larger force, comprising HMS *King George V, Victorious, Illustrious, Indomitable, Indefatigable, Argonaut, Ceylon, Euryalus* and *Black Prince,* with the destroyers *Grenville, Undine, Ursa, Undaunted, Wager, Kempenfelt, Wakeful, Whirlwind, Whelp* (First Lieut., Philip Mountbatten) and *Wessex* made two attacks against the refineries at Palembang. Aircraft losses were high and  nine pilots were taken prisoner. They were tortured in Singapore, and beheaded on August 20, 1945 *after* the war had ended. So much for Japanese chivalry.

The fleet did not return to Trincomallee following the attack on Palembang but sailed for Sydney, arriving there on February 10 to an exuberant reception from the Australians.

The fierce and protracted fight for Iwo Jima increased the urgency of assigning Admiral Fraser's ships to the American Fifth Fleet in time for them to take part in the invasion of Okinawa. Many details were worked out at Sydney in February. The BPF had confidence in itself, based on experience gained in the actions of the previous months, but there was one essential component that remained to be perfected: supply and repair of a fleet at sea. A warship's endurance at sea is limited by her expenditure of fuel and, where action had been joined, her expenditure of ammunition. In the days of Empire, the Royal Navy established fuelling stations, ammunition dumps and repair depots at strategic spots around the globe: from the Falklands to the West Indies to Halifax; from Gibraltar to Aden to Singapore to Sydney to Esquimalt. HM ships were never more than a few days' steaming from one of these bases, The United States Navy, operating in the vast Pacific Ocean with no far-flung colonies in which to establish naval bases, solved its supply problem by the formation of the Fleet Train - a column of tankers, ammunition carriers, supply ships and repair ships stretching from some distant shore base to rendezvous points just a few hours steaming from the operational area of a strike force. With proper organization of the Fleet Train (and the Americans had perfected the organization), a strike force could remain at sea for months on end.

Rear-Admiral Fisher RN was given the responsibility of creating a Fleet Train for the BPF, based on Sydney with a forward base at Manus. Although the British did their best, their Fleet Train never approached the efficiency of the Americans, to whom in the future British commanders would have to appeal more than once to cover deficiencies.

The British warships, now designated Task Force 113, with Vice-Admiral Bernard Rawling's pennant in *King George V*, left Sydney for Manus on February 28, 1945. The Fleet Train, as Task Force 112, sailed independently. TF 113 arrived at Manus March 7 and anchored for ten days, becoming acquainted with prickly heat, boils and a shortage of fresh water. (The distillery ship had been held up at Sydney, the first deficiency in the Fleet Train.) The base commander at Manus, Commodore Boak USN, was most helpful, giving the Task Force full use of Panam Island. At the end of the ten days, King's grudging assignment of the BPF to Nimitz's command for the attack on Okinawa arrived at Manus. The Fleet Train departed March 17, followed by the Task Force next morning, to join the American Fifth Fleet - 385 warships and 828 assault craft - at Ulithi in the Carolines. At Ulithi, Task Force 113 was redesignated Task Force 57: the battleships HMS *King George V* and *Howe*; aircraft carriers HMS *Indefatigable, Indomitable, Illustrious* and *Victorious*; cruisers HMS *Argonaut, Black Prince* and *Swiftsure,* HMNZS *Gambia* and *Euryalus*; destroyers *Grenville, Ulster, Undine, Urania, Undaunted, Quickmatch, Quiberon, Wagner, Queensborough, Quality, Whelp* and *Wager.*

Landings on Okinawa began at 0830 on April 1, although the offensive had been foreshadowed several days earlier with mine clearing, bombarding and landings on adjacent small islands. Because Task Force 57 was relatively untried in battle, Nimitz assigned to it the neutralization of enemy airfields on Sakashimo Gunto and Formosa. With these fields unusable, the invading forces on Okinawa would be spared air attacks from the southwest.

Task Force 57 got right to work; its first strikes were flown on March 26; it had its first "Red Alert" on April 1, when a kamikaze struck *Indefatigable's* island*, and a 500lb bomb hit *Ulster*. The carrier suffered little damage and remained operational, but the destroyer had to be towed by HMNZS *Gambia* to Leyte for repairs.

Task Force 57 was the Royal Navy's reincarnation in the Pacific. To atone in some measure for the defeats of 1941/2, its aim was to fight against Japan to the war's successful end. It was this small fleet (as compared to the huge USN fleets) that HMCS *Uganda* was hastening to join.

---

* An aircraft carrier's superstructure.

1.  Edwyn Gray, *Operation Pacific, The Royal Navy's War Against Japan 1941 - 1945.* (Annapolis, Maryland: Naval Institute Press, 1989)

2.  Geoffrey Bennett, *Naval Battles of World War II* (London: Batsford, 1975) 175

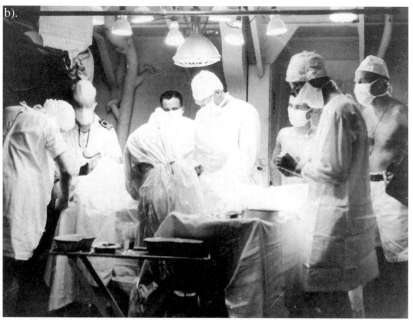

*a). <u>Uganda's</u> bakery. The ship's bread had a truly international recipe, with ingredients from all over the world.*

*b). Surgery in <u>Uganda's</u> sick bay. The ship had well equipped medical and dental facilities.*

## 13. HMCS UGANDA GETS INTO THE WAR.


While *Uganda* awaited transit of Great Bitter Lake on the Suez Canal USS *Quincy*, accompanied by USS *Murphy*, came through, steaming north. The sight of *Quincy* took Vernon back to the tense days and nights of June 1944 - of *Quincy* close astern as *Glasgow* led the way towards the landing beaches; of *Quincy* dodging in and out of smoke off Cherbourg as German straddling fire came down; the damage to *Glasgow*, and her wounded crew. It is understandable that, as *Uganda* got under way, he pondered what lay ahead for him and his ship across the wide Pacific.

The dug channel of the Suez Canal resumes at the southern end of Great Bitter Lake, continuing through Little Bitter Lake and on to Suez, which *Uganda* reached at 1600. Passage of the Canal had taken just over ten hours, at an average speed of ten knots.

That night *Uganda* cleared the Gulf of Suez and entered the Red Sea. The heat increased apace. Vernon's cruising station was "Captain of the Side" , a rather grand title for a Leading Seaman who oversaw a working party detailed to keep a portion of the main deck and the ship's side clean and tidy. The work was not onerous, and gave ample time to observe sharks breaking the surface and flying fish skimming the calm water. But these sights could pall, and with time on his hands, Vernon liked to be on the move. Ship's Standing Orders concerning movement were quite specific:

*6.PUNCTUAL ATTENDANCE AT PLACE OF DUTY - Every man is personally responsible on all occasions for his own punctual attendance at his place of duty.*

*7.PERMISSION TO LEAVE WORK - A man is always to ask permission before leaving his work.*

Vernon understood these orders well and obeyed them fully. But in a ship's routine there are long periods of time when there is really little to do. Officers generally abhor idleness, and are notoriously ingenious in finding work for idle hands; if an officer observed a man idling, he was sure to put him to some task, often trifling, just to keep him at work. Vernon had perfected a technique whereby he avoided such assignments while giving him free access to other parts of the ship. At times, when keeping up the appearance of having work to do was too difficult, he would go for a walk about the ship for a change of scene and a word with a shipmate. He had discovered that if he went on these unauthorized expeditions carrying a rope's end and looking seriously preoccupied, he was never challenged by an officer. Indeed, so well did he play his part that he acquired an unwarranted reputation as a diligent seaman, always doing more than strict duty required of him! Later, when the daily burning of confidential documents was added to his duties, he had a hideaway in the incinerator flat close to the main funnel, which he could use as a base for his forays about the ship.

As *Uganda* approached Aden, in the narrowing sea between Yemen and Eritrea, Vernon's fascination with flying fish gave way to interest in the increasingly heavy dhow traffic. These one-masted cumbersome looking vessels, with their single lateen sail, were a trademark of Arabian waters, carrying all manner of cargoes. When *Uganda* arrived at Aden at 0700, February 17, the harbour was full of them.

After the Suez Canal had been built, the Royal Navy established a coaling station at Aden. Unprepossessingly desolate and hot, it was never a popular spot. At some point in time a Pipe Major in a Highland regiment, perhaps garrisoned in Aden, or maybe just passing through on the way to or from India, immortalized the place by composing a march entitled "The Barren Rocks of Aden". It was a tune Vernon knew, and could play on his mouth organ. He does not remember having the tune in mind that day, but at least he got to see "the barren rocks". He was among the lucky ones to receive shore leave for a guided tour of the bazaars, where each street had its own trade or craft: silversmiths on one street, wood carvers on another, and so on. He saw the many cafes where men drank coffee and chewed gat, and he toured a magnificent garden complex which, he was told, had once belonged to the Queen of Sheba, she who travelled such a great distance to learn the wisdom of Solomon.

The stay in Aden was brief. At 1800 *Uganda* proceeded for Colombo, steaming eastward across the Gulf of Aden, passing Socota Island, into the Arabian Sea, and thence southerly into the Indian Ocean on course to Ceylon. The air temperature on leaving Aden was 84F, the sea temperature 82F. Proceeding closed up, it was very hot.

By now everyone knew that *Uganda* was not suited to tropical service. Ventilation was inadequate; the mess decks were deserted by all who did not have to stay below. Hammocks were seldom slung; hands slept on deck wherever they could claim a space. There was never enough fresh water. If all suffered, the stokers like Roy Campbell fared the worst. Temperatures of 140F were common in the boiler rooms, where the men worked in the elevated pressure of forced draft. To burn the fuel oil cleanly and show no smoke, huge volumes of air had to be forced into the boiler rooms, which could be entered or exited only through double-doored airlocks. This hellish place was one of the few parts of the ship Vernon never visited during his occasional unofficial rounds.

Chefs and galley hands fared only marginally better than the stokers. With ovens, stoves and steam jackets all operating, temperatures in the galley were perhaps ten degrees below those in the boiler rooms. This heat did not deter Vernon who knew that in the galley, especially if Francis Carragher was on duty, there might be some "pickings" if one were discreet.

Four and a half day's steaming brought the ship to Colombo on February 22. The air temperature was 90F, the sea temperature 84F. A few hours shore leave was granted. It was hotter than most of *Uganda's* people had ever experienced and there were smells that none of them could identify. But the sailors had money to spend, having been paid at sea a couple of days previously. Vernon bought a wooden smoking set: a carved elephant's foot ashtray, with genuine ivory toes, mounted on a base in the shape of the island of Ceylon. The wood was reputed to be teak, but he never knew for sure!

Shopping and sightseeing done, some ratings walked four miles to the Fleet Club for a decent meal and a cold beer, making the return journey by rickshaw, another novel experience. Others found their way to a cinema, purchasing box seats with overhead fans, a luxury undreamed of in their overheated ship. As a special event, some WRENS* were invited on board for tea and a dance in the hangar, but it was mostly the officers who entertained them. Only a few lucky ratings (Vernon not one) got to meet them.

Colombo was not all play. There was work to do: taking on provisions; loading construction materials; and stowing a ton of fresh pineapples for delivery to the Cocos Islands. All the lumber would get to its destination, but almost half the pineapples disappeared during the voyage. Their fate was less than mysterious: the food on *Uganda* had not improved. As the ship was technically on loan from the RN to the RCN, the rations were RN, and they were poor quality. Small wonder that fresh pineapples had a brief life expectancy, or that entire cases of tinned fruit could be "lost" during provisioning. The least larcenous matelot, tired of reconstituted dried provisions, could not resist a treat of tasty fruit.

At 1030 on February 24 *Uganda* left Colombo bound for Fremantle via the Cocos Islands. Fifteen Royal Air Force officers had come on board as passengers to the Islands, where an airbase was being prepared. One of the crew was left behind in the RN Hospital to be operated on for appendicitis. Had his attack occurred at sea, an emergency operation could have been performed in the ship's sick bay, but the better facilities ashore were preferable; after convalescence the patient could catch up with the ship. *Uganda* had a well equipped surgery, including an X-ray machine, and a dental office, too. Three navy surgeons and an army dentist were resonsible for these facilities, with staffs of non-commissioned attendants to help.

When well clear of harbour, the A.A. guns' crews were closed up for a practice shoot, to keep them sharp as they steamed closer to hostile waters. It would not do for them to lose the "edge" that they had developed during and since workups.

On February 25, at 2036.5, *Uganda's* position was longitude 85 degrees 25 minutes east, latitude 0. The ship was on the Equator. The first time he "crosses the line" is a significant event in a sailor's life. Regardless of his years at sea, he remains a landlubber in the eyes of Neptune, Ruler of the Deep, until he crosses the Equator. On such an occasion King Neptune, with members of his court, may come on board to elevate landlubbers in the ship to the full status of "courtier". In anticipation of *Uganda's* crossing, King Neptune held court on board at 1500. Under the direction of his courtiers amongst the crew, two canvas tanks, twelve feet square by eight feet deep, were constructed on the main deck. Filled with sea water, they became dunking pools for receiving the initiates. The formalities of admission to court included seating the candidate seaman on a legless chair at the edge of the pool; smearing his face with grease which was then shaved off by a

---

Womens Royal Naval Service.

# H·M·C·S· UGANDA

**Greetings** Know ye: that in this the 25th day of February I have deigned to hold my court upon the decks of the good ship H.M.C.S. UGANDA in Latitude 0° and Longitude 85° 25' E.............

Be it known that on this day *Vernon Drake* a landlubber and minion of Terrestial Rulers hath found favour in my eyes:.............

Wherefore it hath pleased me to grant this mortal admission to the most noble fellowship of the High Seas whereby alone is secured the perpetual benefits vouchsafed the Denizens of the Deep.........

Be it Remembered that henceforth this; my subject, shall come and go upon my seas, honoured by all my servants which do sail thereon and all my creatures which do swim therein or creep upon the bottom thereof.........................

Given under my Fin and Seal this 25th. day of February 1945

*Neptunus Rex.*

Attest *E. R. Mainguay* Capt.

CHARLESTON
HALIFAX
SCAPA FLOW
NEWCASTLE
GREENOCK
GIBRALTAR
MALTA
ALEXANDRIA
SUEZ
ADEN
COLOMBO
FREEMANTLE
SYDNEY
MANUS
LEYTE
FORMOSA
MIYAKO
SAKISHIMA
TRUK
ADMIRALTY IS.

UGANDA

*Facsimile of the certificate presented to those of <u>Uganda's</u> crew who crossed the Equator for the first time, on February 25th, 1945. These must have been made up some time after the event, as the panel at the bottom lists many ports and destinations not visited until later in the voyage. Vernon Drake does not have his certificate.*

huge, roughly-wielded wooden razor; and forcing him to swallow a foul tasting concoction. A list of misdemeanours - genuine or fabricated - was read out against him, an incomprehensible incantation was muttered over him and finally, with a backward tip of the chair, he was dunked in the tank. No landlubber member of the ship's company, from the Captain to the youngest Ordinary Seaman, was exempt from the ceremony, unless on irreplaceable duty. Hilarity and horse play prevailed throughout, and some time later each new courtier received a certificate attesting to his elevated status.

At first light on the 28th the Cocos Islands were visible on the horizon. By 0835 *Uganda* had dropped anchor off this cluster of tiny coral islands which lie 1150 miles southwest of Singapore. To one crew member they appeared to be "total jungle surrounded by coral", but looks can be deceiving. The islands were (and to some extent still are) copra islands; the "jungle" which the sailor saw was, in part at least, the coconut groves which yielded the copra. The building materials, the reduced consignment of pineapples and the RAF passengers were disembarked by lighter over water so clear that hammerhead sharks could be seen lazing about near the bottom. There was no shore leave, but the ship's company did receive some welcome visitors from ashore. The islands' garrison included a battalion of the King's African Rifles from Uganda, and during the stop a number of these askari* came on board the warship named for their country. The blackness of their skin, their immaculate uniforms and their fine military bearing made a profound impression on Vernon.

*Uganda* weighed and proceeded for Fremantle at 1500. As the ship climbed the southern latitudes, the air became noticeably cooler, and life on board correspondingly more comfortable. To the night watch on the bridge, and to stargazers anywhere on board, the trademark constellation of the southern hemisphere, the Southern Cross, now serenely dominated the night sky. The weather was favourable, and the only interruption to the daily routine was a kit muster. *Uganda* reached Fremantle at 1800 on March 4. The submarine spares carried all the way from Greenock were unloaded, and the ship's company granted shore leave by watches. No-one would ever forget the limitless hospitality of the Australians. Each crew member received a ditty bag containing sundry articles useful to a seaman, such as sewing kits, razor blades and writing materials. And then there was the food: fresh fruits and vegetables; thick steaks; and real ice cream! Not least of all was the freedom to stroll the streets and to exchange the fuggy confines of the messdecks for the sweet Australian air.

The Aussies' welcoming plans included a dance and reception for the evening of March 5, but at 1230 that day *Uganda* had to leave for Sydney. Again, according to pattern, the anti-aircraft guns - 4-inch and pom-pom - exercised against sleeve and drogue targets once the ship was clear of the land. It turned much cooler the next day, and the Indian Ocean offered a taste of its rough weather as *Uganda* steamed across the Great Australian Bight. Seas were breaking over the fo'c'sle and white water was flying high as *Uganda* steered for Bass

---

* "soldiers", in Swahili, the common language of East Africa.

Strait and the Tasman Sea. A northerly course through the Tasman waters brought the ship to Sydney on March 10. Rounding South Head and entering the channel, she passed under Sydney Bridge to tie up at the dockyard by 0845. That afternoon the aircraft carrier HMS *Formidable* entered harbour, but few on board *Uganda*, with the possible exception of the officers, realized how closely the two ships would be working together in a few weeks.

As it was still quite warm in the late Australian summer, the first order of the day was to rig the awnings - another first for these northern sailors. Sydney was Fremantle on a grander scale: warm hospitality, great food and new sights in a big city atmosphere. Over the next few days the entire ship's company, by watches, received long daily leaves ashore. Some fortunate ones, such as Robert Cross, even managed a "forty-eight", time enough to find a nice girl.[1] Vernon had no success in this regard if, indeed, he tried, but Robert and his buddy Tye did quite well. They met "the two Betty's", who took them home to meet their parents and have tea. Over the course of *Uganda's* stay in port the four young people went sightseeing, attended the cinema and enjoyed good food. That the girls lived six miles from the dockyard, and missing the last tram meant a long walk back to the ship bothered the boys not at all. Unfortunately, when the ship was opened to visitors on the afternoon of March 23, Roy and Tye both had to work and could not invite their new friends on board.

Joe LeClair and a friend were fortunate to meet a farmer who took the boys to his spread outside Sydney.[2] During the day he took the Canadians over his vast acreage; in the evening, he drove them back to the city. Before parting with them he asked, "How are you fixed, lads?" meaning, have you lots of money? Of course they hadn't, and the big-hearted Australian made sure that they would not go cash shy.

Not all leave was spent quite so romantically or so comfortably. Sailors from *Uganda* would encounter RN sailors ashore (from HMS *Newfoundland* especially). During these encounters, comparisons of respective ships and navies would inevitably lead to fisticuffs. Vernon claims that he and others like him, who had served in British ships, took no part in these small bare knuckle wars between "friends" and allies. The Sydney police understood the psychology of these battles quite well; when one broke out, they simply cordoned off the area and let the fight proceed until honour was served or the combatants tired themselves out. There was no calling the Shore Patrol, hence no Reports and no punishments.

Midway through the stay in Sydney, Admiral Sir Bruce Fraser, Commander-in-Chief of the British Pacific Fleet, came on board to brief *Uganda's* officers on their future duties. Another distinguished visitor was Canada's High Commissioner to Australia, Mr. Justice T.C.Davis, but of course Vernon saw little of such exalted persons.

*Uganda* left Sydney at 1300, March 24, with *Formidable* and the destroyers HMS *Ursa* and *Urchin*. Their destination was Manus; the course was northerly through the Coral Sea and the Solomon Sea, traversing the gap between New Ireland and Bougainville to gain the Pacific Ocean. An alteration westerly then

116

set a course for Manus, which *Uganda* reached on the sixth day out of Sydney, at 0845, to secure alongside USS *Trinity*. It was Good Friday, March 30 1945.

It had not been an idle pleasure cruise from Sydney. The ships were in waters over which war had passed and were bound for an operational theatre. Gunnery practice was continued and certain fleet manoeuvers exercised. On March 27 , for example, a towing exercise was carried out with *Formidable*. *Uganda* closed the carrier and streamed the light grass line by which the heavy towing hawser would in turn be passed between ships. The exercise was complete except for the actual tow. Ships were not going to stop unnecessarily in these waters where there was still the remote possibility of a lurking enemy submarine.

The voyage had taken *Uganda* from 35 degrees south latitude across the Tropic of Capricorn to just under 2 degrees south of the equator, from the temperate coolness of the Tasman Sea to the equatorial heat. Despite the heat, there was work to do: in the afternoon a consignment of jeeps was unloaded to an LC(T) alongside to be ferried ashore. While the duty watch was toiling at this task *Formidable* and *Urchin* arrived.

It is doubtful whether anyone in *Uganda*, with the possible exception of an officer or two, had ever heard of Manus, or of the Admiralty Islands for that matter. The Admiralty group is clustered just below the Equator, north of New Guinea and west of the Bismarck Archipelago. Manus is the largest of the islands, measuring about fifty miles long by seventeen miles wide, with a central mountainous spine rising to 2,356 feet. An annual rainfall of 150 inches spawns numerous short, swift rivers which cascade off the mountain slopes to water a flat, muddy coastal plain where large coconut plantations flourish. In prewar times the islands were administered by Britain. As part of the Japanese occupation of the Admiralty Islands, a small force landed on Manus April 6, 1942, establishing defensive positions in the mountains. Recovery of the islands from the Japanese began February 29, 1944, when Americans invaded Los Negros Island. On March 15 the U.S. 8th Cavalry landed on Manus, meeting determined resistance from the well entrenched Japanese. It was not until May 5 that the last enemy holdouts were mopped up. Immediately after securing the island the Americans began constructing the naval base and anchorage where *Uganda* and her companions were now anchored. In the months ahead the ship's company would get to know the place a little better, but this first visit was brief. On the last day of March *Uganda* left Manus for Leyte Gulf in the Philippines, the advance base of Task Force 57.

Sometime during the first night at sea, *Uganda* crossed the Equator on her northward course, but this time King Neptune did not stir from his deep sea lair. On April 2 the ship's company was saddened by the death, from natural causes, of Leading Stoker Phillips. In the presence of his shipmates in solemn formation on the quarterdeck, the Padre read the Burial Service, the Honour Guard fired a volley and Phillips' body was committed to the deep. That same day, too, there was a timely reminder of what lay ahead: an aircraft alert was sounded, but no plane was seen. On April 3, a practice shoot was carried out with *Urchin*. The

117

next day land was sighted at 1000 and by 1700 the ships were in Leyte Gulf.

It was here that General MacArthur had made good on his pledge, "I shall return". On October 20, 1944, somewhere near Tacloban, the General, his aides and Philippine President Osmana waded ashore from a landing craft while cameramen filmed every stride. It was just a few hours after General Krueger's 6th Army had begun the assault that was to reclaim the Philippines from the Japanese.

Fully aware that the attack was coming, the Japanese had made elaborate plans to counter it. Admiral Toyoda had mapped out a naval strategy by which, in spite of American superiority in the air and on the surface, he hoped that the Imperial Japanese Navy would win a great victory and save the Philippines for the Emperor.

The Americans had at their disposal thirty-two heavy, light and escort-type carriers; six fast, modern battleships; six older, slower battleships; nine heavy cruisers; fourteen light cruisers; one hundred destroyers; twenty-two submarines; and forty-nine reconnaissance vessels. Toyoda's forces were much smaller, but included the world's two largest battleships, the 72,800 tons *Musashi* and *Yamato*, and a completely new weapon, the Kamikaze or "Divine Wind", a corps of volunteer pilots pledged to crash their planes in suicidal attacks against American shipping.

Toyoda deployed his ships in two groups: seven carriers, three light cruisers and eight destroyers were to act as a decoy fleet to draw off the bulk of the American fleet, thereby exposing their amphibious landing force to destruction by his main fleet, comprising seven battleships, eleven heavy cruisers, five light cruisers, twenty-five destroyers and eleven submarines, backed up by 800 land-based planes and 116 carrier-based aircraft. It is doubtful whether this strategy could have been successful under the best of circumstances; in the event it proved disastrous for the Japanese.

The battle lasted from October 23 to October 25. When it was over, the Japanese had lost three battleships, including *Musashi*, four carriers, six heavy cruisers, four light cruisers, ten destroyers and some lesser vessels. American losses were one light carrier, two escort carriers, four destroyers and two submarines, plus many ships damaged, often by kamikaze attack.[3] How the fortunes of the war in the Pacific had changed!

Few of the Canadians in Leyte Gulf on April 4, 1945 reflected on these momentous events. There were more immediate considerations, including a stand-to to repel aircraft at 2100, although no planes came over. There were supplies to be taken on board, including disposable gas tanks for carrier-based Seafires, to extend their range.

Task Force 57, which they had come to join, was not "at home", but was off bombarding some place called Sakishima Gunto. Clearly, a whole new geography would have to be learned! Loading completed, *Uganda* left Leyte at 1300 on the 6th to join the Fleet, all hands anticipating action at last.

1. Robert Cross, Personal Diary.
2. Joe LeClair, Recorded conversation.
3. Cesare Salmaggi and Alfredo Pallavisini, 2194 Days of War. (New York: Gallery Books, 1979) 608 - 610.

*Uganda in line astern of HMS Formidable.*

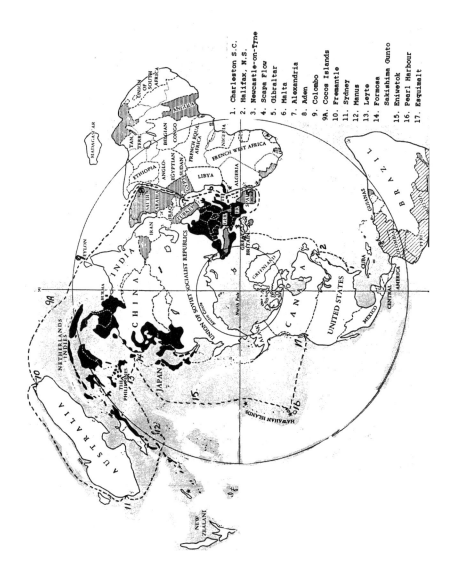

1. Charleston S.C.
2. Halifax, N.S.
3. Newcastle-on-Tyne
4. Scapa Flow
5. Gibraltar
6. Malta
7. Alexandria
8. Aden
9. Colombo
9A. Cocos Islands
10. Fremantle
11. Sydney
12. Manus
13. Leyte
14. Formosa
Sakishima Gunto
15. Eniwetok
16. Pearl Harbour
17. Esquimalt

*Cruise of H.M.C.S. Uganda (Excluding Operations) Oct. 24, 1944 - Aug. 10, 1945.*

# 14. ONE HOT ICEBERG.

The island of Okinawa lies just 350 miles from the nearest of the Japanese home islands. Pursuant to their "island by island" strategy of rolling back Japanese aggression in the Pacific, the Americans had decided as early as October 1944 to invade Okinawa. The landing and subsequent naval support of the invasion forces was code named Operation "Iceberg". Admiral Raymond Spruance, one of the heroes of Midway and now commander of the American Fifth Fleet, was put in charge of "Iceberg". Months of planning and preparation followed. On April 1 1945, before first light, a fleet of some 1300 ships converged on Okinawa. Among them were no fewer than ten battleships, including USS *Texas*, *Nevada* and *Arkansas* back in the Pacific after their participation in the invasion of Normandy. Their 14-inch guns contributed to a naval bombardment ahead of the landing force along an eight mile stretch of Okinawan beach.

Task Force 57 was not assigned to the Okinawa landings directly. Admiral Spruance detailed it to attack and neutralize airfields on Sakishima Gunto, thereby preventing aircraft from using these fields to attack the invasion forces on and off the Okinawa beaches.

Sakishima Gunto is a group of islands in the Ryukyu chain, which arcs southwesterly from Kyushu towards Formosa (Taiwan), roughly halfway between Formosa and Okinawa. The principal islands are Iriomoto, Ishigaki and Miyako. Kamikazes and conventional fighters and bombers used airfields on these islands as home bases or as fuelling stops en route from Formosa, for attacks on Okinawa or Allied ships at sea. Task Force 57's role of containment introduced *Uganda's* sailors to a completely new style of naval warfare. Those experienced in convoy duty, and veterans of independent actions in detached ships, now had to adjust to their ships being handmaidens to aircraft carriers.

The "heart" of the Task Force was the fast aircraft carriers -HMS *Illustrious, Indefatigable, Indomitable* and *Victorious*. All the other ships of the Force, from the great battleships to the nimble destroyers, were to support them: adding to their anti-aircraft defense; screening them from submarine or surface attack; recovering their downed pilots; providing advance warning of impending air attack. Vice Admiral Sir Bernard Rawlings' job was to get the fleet to an operations area within aircraft striking range of Sakishima so that Rear Admiral Sir Philip Vian could launch his Avengers, Corsairs and Seafires against the enemy. In practice this meant approaching within about two hundred miles of the coast, which put the ships within range of enemy bombers and torpedo planes. In order to have as much warning as possible of an enemy's approach, "picket ships" - cruisers and/or destroyers with the best radar - were stationed some twenty-five miles in advance of the fleet, in the direction from which an attack could be expected. Crews on picket ships, being in the front line, as it were, felt exposed and vulnerable. American radar pickets off Okinawa suffered badly; the fact that Task Force 57's pickets were generally ignored by the enemy did not lessen the tension that went with the duty.

Launching (flying off) and recovering (flying on) aircraft required the carriers to steam at high speed into the prevailing wind, to maximize lift for the planes on takeoff and airbraking on landing. When the carriers, which were at the centre of the fleet, turned into the wind, the other ships on station around them had to turn with them. Such manoeuvering was costly on fuel. Moreover, flying from an aircraft carrier was extremely hazardous. In every operation planes were lost to enemy action and by accidents on takeoff and landing. For these and other reasons, Rawlings' plan was to keep the Task Force in the operations area for two days of strikes, then to retire for two days to a fuelling and supply area, out of range of enemy aircraft, where the Task Force could meet its Fleet Train. While TF 57 was away from operations, an American force maintained attacks on the targets.

Task Force 57 had three fuelling areas, 500 or more miles to the southeast of Sakishima Gunto. Merely coordinates on the ocean chart, the areas were designated "Cootie" (most easterly), "Midge" (southeasterly) and "Mosquito" (southwesterly). At one of these areas all the ships would effect necessary minor repairs and replenish their fuel, ammunition and food supplies from the Fleet Train. The carriers, in addition, would acquire replacement aircraft and a fresh supply of aviation gasoline. With luck, there might be mail from home, too.

*Uganda* arrived at "Cootie" on April 7, accompanied by tankers. TF 57 was off "at the front" flying strikes against Sakishima Gunto, but at 0630 the next day the ships returned. Crews on *Uganda, Urchin* and *Ursa* had their first glimpse of the fleet: four carriers, two battleships and eighteen cruisers and destroyers. Later in the day *Uganda* transferred the gas tanks to *Victorious* (they would be attached to her Seafires, to extend the operational range of these superb fighters) and aviation oil to *Illustrious*. After their own ship was topped up with fuel from the tanker *Cedardale*, the Canadians had time to observe the activities around them. Amongst other things, Vernon witnessed his first plane crash, a token of things to come, when a replacement aircraft failed in a landing attempt on its carrier.

They learned, too, that they had missed some hot action. Just a week earlier, on the first day of the Okinawa invasion, the Task Force had been attacked by Japanese aircraft. *Indomitable* was strafed, *Indefatigable* was kamikazed, and *Victorious* was near-missed by a "kk", as was *Ulster* by a bomb. Somewhat shaken, the Task Force had withdrawn to "Midge" to refuel and repair over April 2 - 5, returning to Operations on the 6th.

Meanwhile, against the U.S. fleet at Okinawa itself, the Japanese initiated Operation TEN-bo (Heavenly Operation) by launching Kikisui 1 (First Floating Chrysanthemum), a force of 350 kamikazes from Formosa. They went first for the radar picket ships (destroyers) and sank two of them; then they attacked the main invasion fleet. Although forty-three American ships were damaged, none were sunk, and three-quarters of the attackers were shot down.

Kamikaze pilots were not the only suicidal subjects of the Sun Emperor. In the afternoon of April 6 the Japanese 2nd Fleet sailed from Tokiyama Bay on Honshu, bound for Okinawa. It was on a suicide mission too, for its ships had only fuel enough for the outward journey - none for the return. As it happened they did not need what little oil they had. American submarines spotted the Japanese before they had cleared the Bungo Strait and at first light on the 7th, American aircraft were searching for them. They found them in the East China Sea; hundreds of carrier-based planes were launched against them. The first wave came in at 1228, the second at 1330, followed by more, the attack continuing until after 1400. Like the Royal Navy three years before, the Japanese now had no air cover, and like the British, they paid dearly. The cruiser *Yahagi* was the first to be sunk followed by the greatest prize of all, the mighty *Yamato* which, bombed and hit by at least seven torpedoes, ceased at 1423 to be the greatest battleship afloat. Four destroyers sunk and two damaged completed the score, against a loss of ten of the 376 American planes delivering the attack.

On April 8 HMS *Swiftsure* and HMNZS *Gambia* (just returned from towing the damaged *Ulster* to Leyte) took *Uganda* on Fleet exercises to show the newcomer the ropes of fleet manoeuvering, signalling and so on. That day, too, orders arrived for a strike against Formosa on the 11th and 12th. It was bad flying weather on the 11th, with clouds and rain; the strikes for that day were cancelled. The sea remained calm, however; indeed, *Uganda* had not had a rough day since leaving Sydney. The gun crews closed up to 2nd degree, as usual, at 0530, in case of an attack, but none came. April 12th was clear. Gun crews again stood-to at daybreak, but there were no attackers. In mid-morning the carriers headed into the wind, the screening ships turning with them, and off flew the planes for strikes against Shenchiku airfield and Hiirun harbour on Formosa.

"Ugandans" learned more about this new kind of warfare: for example, that whenever bombers and their escorting fighters took off and returned, a special flight of fighters, the Combat Air Patrol (CAP, for short) was aloft and ranging about to intercept any enemy intruders. With the return of the strike they heard for the first time, too, the broadcast results of the aircraft actions; in this instance, extensive damage to runways and harbour installations, and fourteen enemy aircraft destroyed on the ground or in the air, against a loss of four Task Force planes. These post-action reports, while not always accurate (later analysis of this action put the score of aircraft lost at six on each side), were judged good for fleet morale, giving the non-carrier sailors some sense of being in the fight against the enemy. Shenchiku was hit again the next day, as was Matsuyama. This time the score was eight for one, with relatively little enemy resistance.

News of President Roosevelt's death reached the fleet before the end of the day. Back at "Cootie" on the 14th, colours were flown at half mast for the last thirty minutes before sunset. HMS *Illustrious*, badly in need of relief, left for Leyte, accompanied by HMS *Urania* and HMAS *Quality*. HMS *Formidable*, with *Kempenfelt* and *Wessex*, arrived to take her place. On *Formidable's* bridge was Captain W. G. Andrews, *Uganda's* skipper when she HMS.

HMCS *Uganda* had become so adept at fuelling at sea that in just two hours alongside *Wave King*, she had topped up her tanks. Good seamanship is required to keep oiler and oilee on parallel courses while fuel is being pumped by the ton through a pulsating hose suspended between them. Vernon often did a trick on the wheel during these manoeuvers, and usually all went well. On one occasion, however (it was May 3, and Vernon does not remember if he was steering!), the ships yawed momentarily, breaking the fuel line. *Uganda's* decks and sides were flooded with a black sticky mess and to make matters worse the broken fuelling gear fouled one of the starboard propellers. The ship had to be stopped while a diver went down to clear the obstruction. It was a tense time, sitting motionless in a potentially hostile sea; not all the sweat was from the heat of the sun! Neither Commander Pullen's remarks, nor the grumbling of the clean-up party would make appropriate reading, and entertaining as the incident might have been for lookers-on, everyone was relieved when the diver completed his task, and way was resumed.

By the April 15, all ships having been replenished, the Task Force departed for the operational area from where, on the 16th, two strikes were flown against Ishigaki and two against Miyako. Enemy resistance to these raids was weak; returning pilots reported aircraft destroyed on the ground, and runways made unserviceable by bomb craters. Craters could be filled in during the dark hours, and it was by no means certain that at least some of the "planes" destroyed on the ground were not dummies. For these and other reasons, three more strikes went out against Miyako on the 17th, before the Task Force withdrew for fuelling. Two days later, the ships were back on operations; on the 20th four attacks went in on Miyako and Ishigaki. They were the Task Force's parting shots before leaving for Leyte, buoyed by a congratulatory signal from Admiral Nimitz. More to the liking of *Uganda's* crew was a delivery of mail via HMS *Crane*, met en route. It was their first word from home for many weeks.

The return to Leyte (San Pedro Gulf) ended 32 days at sea, and gave the crews a much needed respite from operations. It did not, however, afford them shore leave, because there were no facilities ashore. For recreation there was swimming over the side, movies and band concerts in the hangar. Recordings by Duke Ellington, Benny Goodman and Glenn Miller, the popular dance orchestras of the time, were played over the ship's P/A system There was a "war canoe" race, in whalers, won by a crew of New Zealanders from *Gambia* because, it was alleged, of a mistake by the coxswain of the Canadian boat. At least, that was the excuse for throwing him overboard after the race!

These diversions could not compensate for the major discomfort of Leyte: the sticky heat. Accumulating heat converted the steel-enclosed spaces of the motionless ship into ovens, making it impossible to sleep below decks. Sleeping on deck was equally impossible because of the sudden, drenching cloudbursts that came down out of nowhere. Calamine ointment was liberally applied against heat rash, and salt pills were a required dietary supplement. Jim Grady[1] got some cooling relief from his personal supply of shaving lotion until the bottle disappeared from his locker. A mess mate later "found" the bottle - empty - and Grady was convinced that the contents were used internally rather than applied externally. As for approved alcoholic beverages, there was beer: six cans per man were brought on board, to be consumed at the rate of one per day, and only on the upper deck.

The "business side" of *Uganda's* life was not neglected. With cooperation from the Americans, A.A. gunnery and aircraft recognition skills were practised. On their first operational stint, *Uganda's* crews had been briefed in the general principle that any fast-flying aircraft over the fleet was probably unfriendly and should be fired upon. It was not unknown, however, for Combat Air Patrol aircraft, in hot pursuit of enemy planes, to come in over the ships, thus presenting the gunners with a dilemma: who was friend and who foe? Aircraft recognition required a keen eye for detail; planes came fast from all angles, and there was no time for consulting a manual of silhouettes to confirm identity.

As usual, the ship required fuel and provisions, and if these could be obtained from the Americans, the work was done more willingly, in spite of the heat. Cigarettes and other comforting goodies were more likely to be obtained from the American than from the British Fleet Train. If provisioning parties recognized a treat such as canned fruit coming on board, the Supply Officer would likely have a deficiency, explicable only as "wastage", at the end of the day. But somewhere in the messdecks, a tasty variation to the plain galley food would be available to those "in the know".

By the end of a hot, wet and not totally restful week, the fleet was provisioned, ammunitioned and oiled. *Indefatigable* had had her damage repaired and by April 30 the ships were under sailing orders. During the last couple of days in Leyte a cloud of rumour drifted through *Uganda* to the effect that the Canadian Government was going to require that all personnel in the Pacific theatre, regardless of their original terms of enlistment, must revolunteer for service against the Japanese. It was further rumoured that anyone who volunteered would be eligible for home leave - some said for thirty days, others claimed to have heard it would be fifty days. It was something for the Canadians to think about as they left Leyte with Task Force 57 on the morning of May 1.

On the second day out *Uganda* practised radar calibration with aircraft from *Victorious*. *Uganda* was equipped with three sets of radar: Type 277, a surface and low warning radar with a range of 25 to 35 miles; Type 283, an air warning radar with a range of 100 miles at 29,000 feet; and Type 293, air and surface target indicating radar with a range of 12 miles. Installed before the ship left Newcastle the previous autumn, these were considered to be state of the art sets; they were not, however, without limitations and required experienced operators for best results. Moreover, the Japanese knew something of the limitations of radar and planned their attacks accordingly, approaching their targets very high or very low so as to avoid radar detection for as long as possible.

Something novel was planned for May 4. The day began with an attack by enemy aircraft (not part of the plan!) at 0545. The planes were easily driven off without causing damage. The Task Force responded with morning bombing raids on Miyako and Ishigaki. It had been decided, whether for tactical purposes or simply to give the crews a feeling of more direct participation in the action, to shell Miyako, as well as bomb it. Accordingly, the First Battle Squadron (*King George V* and *Howe*) and the Fourth Cruiser Squadron (*Black Prince, Euryalus, Swiftsure, Gambia* and *Uganda*) with the Twenty-fifth Destroyer Flotilla

(*Grenville, Ursa, Undine, Urchin, Urania* and *Undaunted*) as screen, had detached from the fleet and taken up position off Miyako Jima. The battleships' 14-inch guns were ranged on Hirara airfield and its A.A. installations 25,000 yards away. The 5.25-inch guns of the light cruisers were to fire airbursts over Nobara airfield from 17,000 yards. The 6-inch guns of the other three cruisers were to fire from 18,000 yards, *Swiftsure's* and *Gambia's* aimed at Nobara, and *Uganda's* at the Sukama airstrip.

The shoot went well under ideal conditions; *Uganda*, in line astern of *Swiftsure* and *Gambia*, opened fire at noon. In fourteen minutes, she lobbed 180 shells into the runways at Sukama. From his action station in the Director tower, rangetaker Joe LeClair with his powerful glasses could see the Japanese scurrying for cover as the first salvoes landed. After that, dust and smoke blotted out his vision.[2] The gunners were jubilant as aerial spotting reported good results. There was no return fire from shore; for Vernon, closed up on a 4-inch, this was a welcome change from Cherbourg!

Back at the carriers, however, all was not well. A signal that *Formidable* had been hit speeded the conclusion of the bombardment; at 1247 the ships turned towards the carriers at twenty-five knots.

When the Bombarding Force detached from the Task Force the carriers were left with eight destroyers, deployed in pairs in line between them, a formation calculated to give maximum supporting anti-aircraft fire in case an attack came in. And come in it did. Shortly after the battleships and cruisers detached, enemy reconnaissance sniffed out the now vulnerable carriers. "Bogeys" from the Formosa-based 1st Air Fleet were not long in penetrating the radar screen and eluding the Combat Air Patrol; at 1131 a bomb hit *Formidable* near her island, penetrating the deck and setting off a fire. A splinter damaged a boiler, slowing the carrier to eighteen knots. With black smoke billowing from the deck fire, and the big ship losing way, things looked bad; shortly, they would go from bad to worse. Three minutes after *Formidable's* first hit, a kamikaze passed through a hail of anti-aircraft fire from forward to aft along *Indomitable's* starboard side. Apparently unscathed, he zoomed into a cloud momentarily, emerging in a steep dive towards *Formidable's* starboard beam. The carrier turned hard in evasive action, just as the attacker was hit and set on fire. He landed, flaming, on the flight deck, but bounced on over the side and into the water. At 1142 *Indomitable* was attacked by another steeply diving "kami", but the gunners had this one's range; hit repeatedly by fire from the carrier and the destroyer *Quality*, he burst into flames and crashed a mere thirty feet off *Indomitable's* starboard bow.

Thus ended the hottest part of the action; planes of the CAP kept any further attackers at bay. The fires on *Formidable* were quickly brought under control and she was capable of twenty-four knots by 1254. It was 1600, however, before her flight deck was usable; her planes returning from the morning strike had to land on the other carriers.

The Japanese planes which pressed home the attack on the carriers were Zekes (carrier-based Zero fighters modified as fighter-bombers and flown from land bases). With a speed in excess of 350 miles per hour, they were difficult targets to hit; to destroy one was a tribute to the A.A. gunners. Jills (torpedo bombers), Judys and Vals (dive bombers) also participated in the attack but these slower craft were all shot down by Seafires and Corsairs from the carriers. One unfortunate Hellcat coming in on *Formidable* for an emergency landing, unaware that she could not receive him, was mistaken for an attacker and shot down by "friendly" fire. The pilot was rescued unhurt but somewhat resentful.

The Bombarding Force closed with the carriers at 1420, after all the excitement had subsided; at 1450 the Task Force was reformed. In the evening the tally of the day's events showed fourteen enemy aircraft destroyed, and pilots lost, against fifteen British (some pilots recovered) plus ten Avengers destroyed in *Formidable's* hangar.

It had been a near thing. Detaching so substantial a portion of the carrier screen could have been disastrous - would have been disastrous, probably, were it not for the armoured flight decks of the British carriers, which made them less vulnerable to the kamikazes. American carriers' flight decks were of teak, which was more easily penetrated, and more readily set afire by kamikaze hits. The relative invulnerability of the Royal Navy ships came with a price, though; tonnage for tonnage, they could carry barely half as many planes as the American ships. As it turned out, the Task Force got off lightly enough, and when, on May 5, the strikes against Miyako encountered no flak, it was clear that the battleships' 14-inchers and the cruisers' lighter guns had done their jobs well.

Back at "Cootie" next day, Captain Mainguy addressed the ship's company:

> *I am asking whether you will, or will not, continue to serve in this ship and fight against the Japanese...until the ship undergoes her first annual refit, or if she is badly smashed up, her first extensive refit...If you agree to stay on, you have to do nothing by way of signing...if you do not agree to stay on...sign a form in my secretary's office between 0800 and 1600 tomorrow, Monday. The form reads, `I hearby certify that I do not volunteer for service in the war against Japan,nor do I volunteer for service in the Pacific theatre of war.*

The Captain continued with details of how the non-volunteers would get home, and went on to say that when they had left, the remaining crew would be asked to sign a volunteer form. Those who did not sign this second form would be relieved in small numbers, whenever possible, all to be gone no later than the next refit. He also confirmed that special leave would be granted to the volunteers, but without details as to how or when.

These intimations were received with mixed feelings in the messes. Quiet soul searching and heated debates followed. As Robert Cross noted, the mess "was no place to live" with the heat, the lack of ventilation, the rats and the cockroaches. The war in Europe was virtually over, but there was no end yet in sight in the Pacific and there was no indication of any improvement in their lot. On the home side of the world, veterans would be returning to their discharges and first crack at post-war jobs while they (with as many or more years of service) would be stuck on the other side of the globe. Some thought, perhaps, that by getting out of *Uganda*, they might be drafted to a better ship in Canada. Many probably felt isolated and unappreciated as Canadians in a Royal Navy fleet (they did not even have a maple leaf on their main funnel, as practically every other RCN ship had). Then, too, there were wives and families to be considered; to commit to a longer stay in the Pacific without consultation with them was a hard decision to make.    Whatever their feelings, whatever their motives, the crew began lining up outside the Captain's office by 0630 the next morning, May 7th. While the Allied world celebrated victory in Europe, 605 officers and ratings of HMCS *Uganda* said, "We've had enough", and signed the non-volunteer form. Vernon was not one of them. He reasoned that, dearly as he would like to be out, the terms of his enlistment was "for the duration" and, quite clearly to him, the war was still on.

Captain Mainguy had been handed a red-hot potato by his political masters back in Canada, and now he had a dilemma on his hands. How could he carry out the terms and conditions outlined to his crew, and hope to maintain the ship's efficiency? His tentative plans to repatriate and replace non-volumteers, outlined to the crew before the vote (borrowing from the RN or the RAN until Canadian replacements could be brought out) seem in hindsight to have been more opti-mistic than realistic, as though he did not expect the vote to turn out as it did. Should he and his senior officers have prepared the ship's company better before this vote? Vernon does not recall receiving any advice or direction from his divi-sional officer, and certainly nothing from the Captain or the Commander. The best that Mainguy could do seems to have been this rather "Gung-ho!" conclud-ing paragraph of his message to his crew from his bridge at 1900, May 6, 1945:

> *I wish to finish by reading a signal from Vice-Admiral of the British Pacific Fleet to the Royal Navy officers and ratings of the Fleet, which I think is worthy of study: "With the end of the war in West coming very close, I know that all of us    must be wishing that our wives, our families, and our friends could feel that we too, were out of the war. I suggest that the best thing we can do to help them in our letters home is to say that together with many thousands from all over the Empire, we with our Allies are going to finish the job off properly so that peace, when it comes, shall be world-wide, and so have a better chance of lasting. The best news of all we can give them is to tell them that we are in good heart. Nothing will count as much as that*[3]

Fraser might well use this rhetoric before his officers and men; he was not under orders to allow his ships' companies to revolunteer! That Captain Mainguy could have thought the Vice-Admiral's advice would "cut it" with Canadians seems at this distance to be simply naive. Captain Mainguy was, by all standards, a fine officer, but aloof from the lower decks, after the manner of the Royal Navy. Not for nothing does Joe LeClair describe his captain as "an aristocrat, you know, away above us".[4] His Executive Officer, Commander Hugh Francis Pullen, relied for his authority more on the strength of naval discipline than on the earned respect of his subordinates. Neither officer was likely to be a positive influence on a crewman's vote.

The war was not going to stop, or even slow down, while a Canadian crew voted on their future participation in it. The Task Force, back in the operational area, flew four strikes against Hirara in the morning. Anticipating enemy aerial attack, *Uganda's* crews were closed up at 0539, but no "bandits" arrived until late afternoon. The first attack came at 1640; despite violent evasive action *Victorious* was hit by a kamikaze whose bomb penetrated the deck near the forward lift. A few minutes later a kamikaze hit the flight deck aft, but bounced off into the water (the armoured flight deck was paying its way, again). There was another one right behind him, diving on *Victorious*, but at the last moment he appeared to shift aim to *Howe*; before he could reach the battleship, however, he exploded in a mass of flame, and crashed astern. The action ended at 1705, when *Formidable* was hit on the after park deck. The resulting explosion and fire could be plainly seen from *Uganda*. The carrier slowed to fifteen knots while the fire was brought under control and extinguished; by 1755 she was operational again.

This was Vernon's, and *Uganda's*, first taste of real action in the Pacific; it had been brief, hectic and noisy. Oerlikons were spitting, pom-poms were pumping, the 4-inch H.A.'s were firing, even the 6-inch guns had a shot. The din was awful; the air was full of flak, and dotted with bursts of smoke. Totally occupied in keeping a steady flow of 60lb fixed ammunition* to his 4-inch gun, Vernon saw little or none of the action. Patrick Horgan, a loading number on one of the pom-poms, had a ringside view from the more exposed mounting of his weapon. When he saw the hit on *Formidable* he was so awestruck that he stopped working and exclaimed, "Did you see that?" The only answer he received was a profane reminder to resume passing the clips of ammunitiion.[5]

Then, as suddenly as it began, the action ceased. Spent shrapnel was still raining down as the surviving attackers withdrew. Seven enemy planes were seen from *Uganda*; six were shot down, including the spectacular flamer astern of *Howe*. Whose guns made the hits was impossible to determine; every ship in the Task Force was flinging hot metal skyward. With the release of tension at the cease fire, the crews simply slumped at the guns, exhausted. It was a dangerous time to be incautious: on one occasion a 4-inch mounting, still under control from the director, trained hard around, jamming and crushing a sailor's foot. On another occasion a 4-inch with a round "up the spout" was cleared by manual firing (standard, if unauthorized, practice to avoid the trouble of handling hot ammunition); a rating standing too close to the gun was caught by the recoil and flung against a steel screen.[6] Rested and with time to reflect, many of the gun crews wondered at the fanaticism of the kamikaze pilots. Vernon and others had seen German pilots and Allied pilots attack with great bravery but they had never seen them use their aircraft as a piloted bomb. Was this a special form of Japanese heroism or was it just plain stupidity? The majority opinion labelled the

---

\* essentially a large rifle cartridge, with projectile and charge in the one container. Most shells were "proximity fused" to explode near a target.

kamikaze pilots "crazy bastards". (There is a story to the effect that, when *Victorious* was hit the first time her captain summed up the situation in a three-word signal to Rear Admiral Vian in the flagship: LITTLE YELLOW BASTARD. Back from *Indomitable* came an equally laconic reply: ARE YOU ADDRESSING ME ?)

At this point, *Formidable* was operational, but only fifteen of her aircraft were serviceable. *Victorious* was also operational, but with a damaged forward elevator she could handle planes very slowly. *Indomitable* was unscathed, but it was Rear Admiral Vian's view, accepted by Vice Admiral Rawlings, that withdrawal to "Cootie" would allow for full assessment of damage, replacement of aircraft, refuelling and restoration to maximum operational capability. At 1950 the Task Force left for the fuelling area.

At "Cootie" on May 10 *Uganda* oiled, exchanged mail and took on stores. The carriers had their damage made good and received replacement aircraft. Meanwhile at command level the experiences of May 4 and 9 were reviewed and new defensive tactics devised. It appeared that the enemy might be locating the fleet by tracking the CAP with their land-based radar and sending their planes in on a low approach to avoid long range detection. As a first measure, it was decided to reposition the radar pickets to the northwest and southwest of the main fleet to provide earlier warning of the enemy's approach. As the carriers were evidently the chosen targets of the attackers, their defence was to be bolstered: the light cruisers would be withdrawn from the screen to closer support of the carriers; carriers and their main supports were to separated by 2,000 yards; and a destroyer was to follow close astern of each carrier for added defence.

These new dispositions went into effect on May 12 when the Task Force returned to the operations area. Whether they were effective in protecting the fleet from enemy action was not clear; that they increased the hazards of navigation within the Task Force was to become apparent some time later.

The immediate effect for *Uganda* was her first assignment to picket duty; with *Wessex* she was stationed just over the horizon, bearing 223 degrees (southwest) from the fleet centre. From her exposed position she monitored strikes going into Ishigaki and Miyako, kept track of the CAP's, marked the return of the strike aircraft and watched for "bogeys" or "bandits". After two days she rejoined the fleet and returned to "Cootie" where there was mail, and the hospital ship *Tjitalengka*, come to pick up casualties.

Improving his defences against kamikazes preoccupied the Admiral. The need for better aircraft recognition was further stressed; the importance of the Air Defense Officer having the best and latest information on the whereabouts of friendly and unfriendly aircraft was emphasized; and finally, A.A. gunners were ordered not to withhold fire pending positive visual identification of the target - fire first, ask questions later. With these orders in place the Task Force returned to operations, striking Miyako and Ishigaki five times on the 16th, and twice more on the 17th. *Uganda* drew picket duty for this tour which ended with return to "Cootie" on the 18th. One aircraft had been lost to enemy action and four by accidents.

Back at "Cootie" a bizarre accident occurred in *Formidable's* hangar: while a Corsair was being serviced its guns unaccountably went off, hitting an Avenger and causing it to explode. The ensuing fire, fuelled by aviation gasoline and ammunition, was very hard to fight. When it was finally brought under control seven Avengers and twenty-one Corsairs had been destroyed. This day had to be one of the best ever for the enemy against TF 57, although there was not a Japanese within several hundred miles!

Losses of aircraft on Operations were to be expected. Planes were shot down over the target, or were damaged and forced to ditch on the return flight to their carrier. Others made it back only to crack up on the flight deck, with varying degrees of damage to themselves, parked aircraft or the ship itself. Excluding the enemy entirely, carrier flying was inherently hazardous. The flight deck was just long enough to allow a fully-laden plane, starting from full power, to become airborne, and too short for a normal landing. Carrier landing was possible only because of two factors: the "batman" who by signalling with hand-held paddles resembling ping-pong bats guided the pilot in his final approach; and by a series of arrestor wires laid across the flight deck. A hook on the plane's tail was supposed to engage one of these wires which, while stretching under the plane's momentum, would bring the machine to a stop. As a last resort, should the arrestor mechanism fail or not be engaged, steel mesh crash barriers could be erected across the deck to intercept the plane. Damage to arrestor apparatus and/or the barrier mechanisms, or the inability of the carrier to steam at speed could abort flying operations.

Scarcely any strike went without loss of aircraft, although many pilots were recovered, but losses from non-operational causes such as the accident in *Formidable's* hangar were the more numerous.

By nightfall of the 18th *Formidable* was operational to the extent that her flight deck was usable, which was not the case in *Victorious* whose arrestor barriers needed repairs. Because of this and the bad weather (continuous rain and low visibility) the replacement aircraft were delayed in flying on, keeping the Task Force at "Cootie" until the evening of May 19. As they departed to the operations area *Uganda's* crew were more concerned over having received no mail than by the fact that their ship had now steamed more than 40,000 miles since commissioning.

Next morning, according to the revised order of battle, the "kk" destroyers took station astern of their carriers in foggy weather. HMS *Quilliam* rammed her carrier, *Indomitable*, with little effect on the carrier, but wrecking her own bow. HMAS *Norman* took the damaged destroyer under stern tow, and *Black Prince* was detached from the screen, first as escort and then as tow. The salvage operation was beyond the warships' capabilities; tugs had to be called. *Weasel* arrived to take the damaged destroyer to "Cootie"; a USN tug, the *Turkey*, took *Quilliam* on to Leyte.

All this untoward activity reduced the day's strikes to one, but on the 21st five attacks were flown: three against Miyako and two against Ishigaki. Again the fleet withdrew to "Cootie"; again there was no mail.

*Formidable* had reached the limits of her endurance; on May 22 she was detached to Manus and thence to Sydney for repairs. *Kempenfelt* and *Whirlwind*, both due for refit, accompanied her as escort. In *Uganda*, as in other ships of the Task Force, many a wistful rating wished it might have been their ship that was getting the break. The next day one of the surviving heroines of the Plate, HMNZS *Achilles*, joined. There was just time to drill her summarily in kamikaze tactics before the Task Force, with only three carriers now, left for operations at 1818.

Despite wet and cloudy weather on the 24th, Rear Admiral Vian launched strikes at Nobara, Hirara and Ishigaki. The next day Miyako was hit three times and Ishigaki twice. These strikes ended TF 57's actions in Operation "Iceberg". *King George V*, *Troubridge*, *Tenacious* and *Termigant* detached for Guam. The remainder of the Task Force retired to "Cootie" for fuelling before proceeding to Manus.

"Iceberg" ran from March 23 to May 30 - 68 days. Strikes were flown from TF 57 on twenty-four of those days, against Formosa and/or Sakishima Gunto. More than 5300 sorties were flown by carrier aircraft; 958 tons of bombs, and 947 rockets were expended. Miyako Jima was bombarded; 200 tons of shells were showered on the enemy. The tactical results were that Japanese airfields on the left flank of the Okinawan invasion were useless to the enemy; 179 enemy aircraft were destroyed or damaged; and almost 200 small vessels were sunk or damaged.

These results were achieved at considerable cost; forty-one flying crew killed or missing in action; forty-four other personnel killed in action; and eighty-three wounded. Two destroyers were severely damaged; three carriers were moderately damaged but never rendered non-operational; two carriers had superficial damage. Two hundred and three aircraft were lost: 112 on operations; twenty-nine shot down by anti-aircraft fire; thirty-two destroyed by kamikaze attack; and thirty burned out in *Formidable's* hangar fire. Of the 112 losses on operations, sixty-one were deck crashes on landing - the same number as were accounted for by direct enemy action. There were eleven kamikaze attacks on the Task Force. Four aircraft were hit by A.A. fire, causing them to miss or bounce off their target; three were hit but crashed into the target ship; one was destroyed by gunfire before reaching its target; and three were probably not hit. There were, of course, no survivors of the kamikazes that were hit. (As one dark wit put it, "You just don't meet experienced kamikaze pilots".) To complete the account, it must be recorded that two friendly aircraft were shot down.

As for the main operation - the capture of Okinawa - that battle raged until June 22. Japanese infantry resisted ferociously from within a tightly constricting perimeter on the southern end of the island, holding every yard of ground to the death. The final tally for gaining Okinawa is in stark contrast to Task Force 57's "scoresheet": 7,613 Americans killed or missing; 31,807 wounded; 36 ships sunk; 368 ships (including 129 warships) damaged; 3038 naval personnel killed or missing, and 6050 wounded.. On the Japanese side, 110,000 soldiers killed ; 7,400 taken prisoner; 1460 kamikaze pilots killed; 7,800 aircraft lost; more than

75,000 civilian casualties. All for one small island well removed from the Japanese home islands.

To a dispassionate observer in June 1945, Japan was beaten. Her Air Force was destroyed; the remnant of her fleet was immobilized in harbour for lack of fuel. The problem was that the Army remained tenacious and as Allied strategists counted the cost of having captured a few distant islands they must have wondered what toll would be exacted when their forces went ashore on the home islands. The grim planning for that day went forward.

1. James Grady, *Recorded conversation.*

2. Joe LeClair, *Recorded conversation.*

3. Stephen Geneja, *The Cruiser Uganda.*

4. Joe LeClair,

5. Patrick Horgan, *Recorded conversation.*

6. James Grady,

a).

b).

c).

*In the Mediteerranean Sea.*
*a). Valetta harbour, Malta. Note the mast of a sunken ship.*
*b). Uganda's sistership, HMS Newfoundland at Alexandria.*
*c). Egyptian boys employed to clean Uganda"s bilges. Dirty work!*

*a). Souvenir of Egypt. A fanciful postcard scene of the Pyramids, with Vernon's picture superimposed. "I do you very nice picture, boss, very cheap!" Proved very popular with sailors on leave.*
*b). Some of Uganda's crew touring the Queen of Sheba's gardens, Aden, February 17, 1945.*

135

*a).* *Crossing the Equator, February 25th, 1945. Captain Mainguy, captive of Neptunus Rex, is led forward for initiation into the sea monarch's court.*

*b). Askari of the King's African Rifles 1st (Uganda) Battalion on board HMCS Uganda, Cocos Islands, February 28, 1945.*

a).

b).

*The aircraft carriers were the nucleus of the Task Force.*
*a). At sunset, a carrier attended by a destroyer and battleship.*
*b). Uganda, a carrier and another escort in line ahead.,*

137

a).

b).

*Meeting the Fleet Train at "Cootie"*
*a). HMS <u>King George V</u> oiling astern of the tanker, <u>Uganda</u> fueling alongside.*
*b). <u>Uganda</u> takes on ammunition – "condensed thunder and lightning".*

a). *Uganda* bombarding Miyako Jima. The smoke is from the 6-inch's, which have just fired. The 4-inch doubles are trained on target, but have not fired.

b). Vernon at Action Stations by a rack of 4-inch "fixed" ammunition. The helmet is to protect against falling shrapnel; the white hood is asbestosized anti-flash gear. An uninflated life belt completes the ensemble.

c). An Avenger bomber returning with part of its tailplane shot away. The arrestor hook is down, indicating that the pilot will attempt a landing on his carrier.

*a). A kamikaze has an aircraft carrier in his sights. The carrier is fighting back with ack-ack fire.*
*b). A kamikaze hits <u>Formidable's</u> flight deck and explodes.*
*c). The resulting fire, mostly burning aviation fuel. It was quickly extinguished.*

## 15. HMCS UGANDA'S FINAL OPERATIONS.

Prior to his departure in *King George V* Vice Admiral Rawlings received the following signal from Admiral Spruance, C-in-C 5th Fleet, USN:

*On the completion of your two months operations as a Task Force of the Fifth Fleet in support of the capture of Okinawa, I wish to express to you and to the officers and men under your command my appreciation of the fine work you have done and the splendid spirit of cooperation with which you have done it. To the American portion of the Fifth Fleet, Task Force 57 has typified the traditions of the Royal Navy.*

Vice Admiral Rawlings replied as follows:

*It will give me great pleasure to pass your generous message to those of the BPF who have had the honour of serving under you during these two months. We are proud to have been able to lend a hand in this crucial operation and we hope to go on doing so until the day of Victory. My one regret is that King George V and I were unable to be at Guam when you returned.*

Vernon does not recall that this exchange of signals was ever broadcast to *Uganda's* people. As a morale raiser, it should have been remembered, but then spirits were high as the ship left for Manus on May 27. The Captain had said that one way or another the non-volunteers would be leaving for Canada by July 15, and the prospects for further operations before then were not great. So, who cared that it grew hotter on the 28th as the ship steamed southwards toward the equator? They were not closed up, and life was lighter. The next day was even better: it was cooler, and it was payday.

When *Uganda's* anchor bit into the sand off Manus the ship had been at sea for sixty-two days, counting the eight days at Leyte. Many ratings had not been ashore since leaving Sydney. In the tropical heat of Manus going ashore required an effort which to some of the more weary seemed hardly worthwhile. But for those who craved shore leave, the Liberty Boat could not arrive soon enough. This conveyance to shore, which regularly made the rounds of the anchored ships, was a retired landing craft whose ensign was a rather the worse-for-wear pair of lady's panties. The delights to which it transported its eager passengers included swimming, lying on the palm-shaded beach, baseball games and even beer, albeit on a ration of two cans per person. The beer was available at Duffy's Tavern, an open-sided tin-roofed shelter close to shading coconut palms near the beach of Peytilus Island.

Conditions, although hot, were ideal - sunny days, calm blue waters and clear nights under the Southern Cross - and if the older (in experience if not in years) preferred to remain on board it was to savour the freedom from stand-to's, to catch up on sleep, and to enjoy some relaxation in discipline. Vernon remembers quiet parties on the darkened fo'c'sle, a little harmonica music and maybe a song or two as a little illicitly hoarded rum was discretely passed.

As if this were not enough, June 1 brought a raise in pay: thirty cents a day for Able Seamen, forty-five for Leading Seamen. What riches! But how to spend the extra income? There was nothing to buy, and nowhere to buy it. The prudent increased their home allotments; the foolhardy (or the optimists) committed their increases to games of chance.

Ever since May 1 the witches' brew of Pacific voluntarism had continued to simmer. Naval Service Headquarters in Ottawa did not accept Captain Mainguy's voting procedure of May 7, insisting by signal of May 23 that only affirmative votes could be taken as indications of willingness to serve. Accordingly, a second ballot was to be conducted by which all personnel must volunteer by signing or be declared non-volunteers.

The signals relative to voluntarism passing between Ottawa and *Uganda* apparently were not being copied to Admiral Fraser. Inasmuch as his command would be seriously affected by *Uganda's* withdrawal, or by the lost efficiency resulting from crew rotation, it seems incredible that Fraser was not kept informed and included in the planning. On May 27 he weighed in with a signal to the Admiralty and NSHQ. It read, in part:

> *...efficiency under present operating conditions cannot be maintained at any rate of dilution which would be consistent with the release of ratings in reasonable time to implement Canadian Government policy.*
>
> *I therefor propose that HMCS Uganda should return to Canada to recommission with volunteers, as I think there is now no alternative. To maintain the number of cruisers in the Task Force at the necessary 6, the earliest she can be spared is mid-July when HMS Argonaut rejoins.*
>
> *That HMCS Uganda should have apparently sailed for the Pacific without knowledge of conditions of service is difficult to understand. The form of the announcement and with many rumours preceding it have placed the C.O. and all on board in a most difficult position. <u>It will have caused a fine ship to be withdrawn from the line for other than operational reasons</u>\* It will cause me difficulty in forming the Fleet into two self-contained Task Groups which I had promised the Americans could be done...*

Lower deck people were not privy to these counsels of the mighty (although Joe LeClair, by virtue of his job in the Commander's office, was often able to reveal the contents of "confidential" signals to select friends). For *Uganda's* ship's company the next event in the sequence took place the following week.

---

\* emphasis mine.

On June 2, 1945, polling booths and ballot boxes were set up on *Uganda's* quarterdeck at Manus. One box was for votes cast in the federal election; one box was for votes cast in an Ontario provincial election; a third box was for the declarations of those who volunteered for Pacific service in the war against Japan. For many of the crew it was their first civil vote; for others their age still denied them their franchise. But all were qualified to vote on the matter of voluntarism. When those votes were tallied, the result was unchanged from May 4: two -thirds of the ship's company said, "We're not PV's*; we're going home."

Shipboard activity increased in the week following the election. Provisions, ammunition and fuel were loaded in preparation for Operation "Inmate", a naval bombardment of air fields on Truk, an island in the Carolines 700 miles northeast of Manus. *Uganda* weighed from Manus at noon on June 12, accompanied by the cruisers HMS *Swiftsure* and *Newfoundland* and HMNZS *Achilles*. During the afternoon the A.A. crews were drilled against sleeve targets, after which the cruisers rendezvoused with HMS *Implacable*. On the 13th the ships simulated bombardment procedures to practise communications with *Implacable's* spotting aircraft. The results were less than perfect.

On the 14th the carrier sent repeated aerial strikes against Truk. *Uganda's* A.A. crews closed up at second degree from 0700, and a Combat Air Patrol of eight Seafires kept vigil aloft. Neither the gun crews nor the aircraft were engaged.

At 0645 on the 15th, the day of the bombardment, Rear Admiral Brind USN transferred his flag to *Uganda*, which thus became the flagship of the operation. By 1000 the Bombarding Force was approaching the barrier reef on the east side of the atoll; the Carrier Force was ten miles farther to the east. Twelve Seafires maintained a CAP over both forces, and an additional six were airborne as spotters. Their pilots, however, were not those with whom the Communications Officers had earlier rehearsed the action. The Bombarding Force was split into three units, each of which was to steam due west towards the reef until it was within range of its target, at which time it would turn parallel with the reef and open fire. *Swiftsure* and *Teazer* were the most northerly; *Achilles, Uganda* and *Tenacious* were in the centre; *Newfoundland* and *Troubridge* were the most southerly. *Uganda's* and *Achilles'* target was Dublon Island, with its oil storage tanks and seaplane base. The range was 20,000 yards; each 6-inch gun had thirty rounds.

Shortly after 1030 the units turned north; at 1034 *Uganda* opened fire, and immediately there were communication problems with the spotters. The guns were, in effect, firing blind. At 1050 fire was checked while the ships turned 180 degrees to starboard to steam back along their tracks. Fire was resumed at 1056, but it could be seen from the Director Tower that the salvos were falling far off the target, landing in the water just north of Eten Island, which was *Newfoundland's* target. Firing ceased at 1110 and the ships withdrew.

---

* Pacific Volunteers.

The gun crews in the turrets, happily blasting away, did not know it, but the attack had been essentially a failure. *Newfoundland* scored some hits but the principal damage to Truk was done by the Avengers and Seafires bombing, rocketing and strafing before and after the shelling. What had gone wrong?

The first contributing factor has been identified already: the pilots in the spotting planes had not exercised with the ships. Secondly, communications overall were very bad. Thirdly, despite lessons learned in Normandy and elsewhere, one spotter was assigned to two ships. The inevitable immediately happened: the spotter confused *Newfoundland's* fall of shot with *Uganda's* and *Achilles'*, calling back the wrong corrections and leading their guns farther off target. Lastly, someone at *Uganda's* plotting table was making his own corrections based on miscalculations. It was all less than glorious, but as the operation was classified as a training exercise the failures were viewed less seriously and the analysis of the debacle presumably led to rectifying some errors.

On Sunday, June 17 *Uganda* was back at Manus where, with short intervals at sea, she would remain for two and a half weeks. On board, the crew was kept busy painting, provisioning and ammunitioning. There were movies and other entertainments in the hangar, including a concert by the combined bands of *Achilles* and *Uganda*, and a dance band from the ship. At sea they practised anti-aircraft gunnery, night engagements, radar calibration and height finding. Ashore, they lazed on the beach, drank their beer allotment, ate their fill of green coconuts and fought with the "Kips". And they waited for mail. And waited. Until, finally, on July 5th, it arrived: fifty bags of mail that had been trying to catch up with them for weeks.

In spite of the entertainment, in spite of the mail, in spite of time ashore, the men were growing restive. The exercises at sea, designed to keep efficiency up, were increasingly tiresome. On June 26, during an exercise, tragedy struck: Petty Officer Joseph Dumont suffered a massive stroke and died at his gun. He was buried at sea the same day. Vernon helped to prepare the weighted hammock which was his shroud and coffin. His pallbearers were all messmates (including Petty Officer Richard Curley from Prince Edward Island). P.O. Dumont's shipmates took up a collection for his wife and ten-year old daughter; their contributions totalled $2124.87, a sum which in those days was the equivalent of almost three year's salary.

The growing discontent in the lower decks fed on uncertainties stemming from the volunteer issue. When were they leaving for home? What leave could they expect? And so on. Inevitably there was friction between the volunteers and the non-volunteers; many of the latter were convinced (quite mistakenly) that Captain Mainguy was prolonging their stay to punish them for not volunteering.

Provisioning and other preparations for sea having been completed, *Uganda* weighed on July 6, leaving Manus to join the U.S. Third Fleet (the former Fifth Fleet, now reclassified and commanded by US Admiral "Bull" Halsey) off Japan. The British fleet which left Manus was designated as Task Force 37, under command of Vice Admiral Rawlings. It comprised the battleship HMS *King George V*; the aircraft carriers HMS *Formidable, Victorious* and

*Implacable;* cruisers HMS *Newfoundland, Black Prince, Euryalus,* HMCS *Uganda,* HMNZS *Achilles* and *Gambia*; destoyers HMS *Grenville, Undine, Urania, Ulysses, Undaunted, Quiberon, Troubridge, Tenacious, Termigant, Terpsichore* and *Teazer.*

The cooler weather at sea, the familiarity of sea routine and mail to read and reread raised flagging spirits somewhat, A good A.A. shoot on Saturday, in which *Uganda's* gunners outshot *Newfoundland's* also helped, but Divisions and church on Sunday did not. Then, in the week that followed, as they crossed the vastness of the Pacific, the sea got up to some of the heaviest weather of the voyage; breasting the long Pacific rollers, *Uganda's* tapering bows flung spray high and wide. On the 12th they began fuelling from the Fleet Train tankers but the heavy seas slowed the process and it was Sunday the 15th before fuelling was completed.

About this time, too, *Uganda* had another fatality on board. Sometime during the early hours of the 12th a nineteen-year old stoker disappeared. He had been sleeping on deck near the torpedo tubes, where there was no railing, and it is assumed that he must have rolled over the side. As soon as he was missed the entire ship was searched, but no trace of him was found.

On July 16, 300 miles southeast of Shikoku Island, TF 37 closed with the American Third Fleet. In *Uganda* only the D Day veterans such as Vernon had ever seen a greater armada, and even for them the Third Fleet was an unforgettable naval spectacle: nine Essex-class carriers; six light carriers; seven battleships; fifteen cruisers; sixty destroyers - ninety-seven ships in all. With the addition of TF 37 a total of 118 warships would carry the war to Japan's home islands.

The first strikes were flown from 250 miles out. The targets for TF 37's aircraft were airfields at Sendai, Matsushima and Masudo. There was no picket duty for *Uganda*; on this operation she was part of the screen. Anti-aircraft crews closed up at 0415, but did not have to fire. Strikes continued the next day against Nobara, Konoiki, Naruto, Miyakawa and Kayori. A bombardment by a portion of the fleet (not including *Uganda*) went badly because rain and fog over the target area prevented spotting.

TF 37 left the operations area on the 19th to refuel. Admiral Halsey expected fuelling to be accomplished according to the same schedule as in his fleet - in one day - but herein he did not know the ways of the British Fleet Train. Not only had he to grant TF 37 two days for fuelling, he had to deal with the following signal from Rawlings:

In respect of HMNZS *Gambia* and *Achilles* and HMCS *Uganda*:
Math. 25, 7 - 8.
On USS *Missouri's* bridge a bible was quickly produced and the reference found:
*Then all these virgins arose and trimmed their lamps. And the*
*foolish said unto the wise, "Give us of your oil, for our lamps have*
*gone out"*
Correctly divining that the Brits didn't have enough oil for their own ships, Halsey's reply was more practical than biblical.

*Foolish - no. Wise - maybe. Virgins - no comment.*
Permission was given to oil from the Americans.

At least there had been mail with the Fleet Train - twenty-six bags of it, but it did not seem to have its usual spirits-raising effect in the rumour-charged messdecks. Word was going around that they would not be leaving after all; that they would be kept on operations so that a British cruiser could leave for refit. And the mail from home brought stories about the publicity being given to the new cruiser HMCS *Ontario* as she prepared for the Pacific at Esquimalt. *Uganda*'s crew could not be blamed for contrasting their quiet departure from Halifax with the alleged fanfare on the west coast. Robert Cross groused in his diary, "We never got a ditty bag from home. No wonder the boys didn't volunteer...if the Old Man has his way we'll sweat to death down here...if he stalls us off again we may as well stay here for good."[1] Cross and his messmates could not know it, but the end was near.

Strikes were flown on July 24 and 25 against Akushi, Fukuyama, Sato and shipping in the Inland Sea. As usual the A.A. crews closed up at dawn to repel aircraft; *Uganda* did not engage at any time, although there were enemy aircraft over the fleet and observers saw some shot down. Also on the 24th the Third Fleet began the destruction of the remnants of the Imperial Japanese Navy in Kure Bay. It took four days. It was America's final revenge for Pearl Harbor and the British were not allowed to participate, which was unfair, for the Royal Navy had its own grievous losses to the Japanese to avenge. But Admiral King's unyielding hatred of the British remained pervasive.

While *Uganda* was fuelling at sea on July 26 word raced through the ship that departure for home was imminent. When fuelling was completed on the 27th, and certain gear had been transferred to HMS *Argonaut* and to attendant destroyers, *Uganda* detached at 2000 for Esquimalt via Eniwetok and Pearl Harbor. At 1600 Task Force 37 had left to proceed to the coast of Honshu for bombardment. Vice-Admiral Rawlings sent a farewell signaL:

*I am very sorry you are leaving us, and I look forward to your return.*

1. Robert Cross, *Personal Diary.*

146

## 16 HOME FROM THE WAR, HOME FROM THE SEA.


On July 28 HMCS *Uganda* cruised an almost empty ocean alone. Never had the Pacific seemed so immense. At 0800 Iwo Jima was a speck of rock on the horizon; later in the day a convoy was sighted. Operations routine was discontinued: there were no more stand-to's, no more anti-aircraft drills. Sunday Divisions were cancelled, and no Divine Service was held; all hands not on watch were allowed to sleep. On the 30th routine was interrupted by a pipe to "Clear Lower Decks" for a locker search. Jim Grady relates the circumstances as follows:[1]

> *Then there's the story of the Colt .45's. The Colts were all in the Gunner's Stores. We looked after them, cleaning them after they were fired, and so on. As far as I know, there were two keys to the Colt locker; [Lieut.] Landymore had one and maybe [Commander] Pullen had the other - I don't know. One day some officers were using them for practice or something and afterwards I went up and got them and cleaned them, and put them back in the locker. Landymore was there when I was putting them in. Next day Landymore says, "Come with me" and we went to Pullen's cabin. "You stay right here" he says, "and don't move". Pullen comes out and Landymore tells him some Colts are missing. I was the last bird there, but Landymore was there too. They put me in the office so I couldn't spread it around the ship that they were missing, and they sent officers and P.O.'s to all the messes in the ship and cleared lower decks one deck at a time. They'd come into the mess and say, "Don't touch anything". They'd get everyone into the middle of the mess and then they'd search all the lockers. They went to every mess deck and never found a Colt .45, but they did find, in the P.O.'s mess, enough liquor to -*

Every conceivable hiding place examined. The missing guns were not found, but all sorts of other contraband besides the hoarded rum was turned up: rounds of ammunition, live and spent; cached food. The live ammunition was returned to Gunner's Stores, the foodstuffs and other illicits were variously dealt with; and the rum went over the side. The latter was perhaps the hardest to part with. The guns were never found, and many denizens of the lower decks were convinced that the search was conducted in the wrong place. "Who", they asked, "took target practice with the handguns?" "Why, the officers", was the answer to their own question. Morale was not improved. In addition to the Colts three pairs of binoculars were also missing. None of the missing objects were found.

On the last day of July, 1945, *Uganda* stopped for seven hours at Eniwetok to fuel. This large multi-island atoll isolated in the northwest corner of the Marshall Islands had yet to catch world attention. In 1948 three atomic bombs would be dropped there; in 1951 four more; and when the first hydrogen bomb was detonated there in 1952, everyone knew the atoll's name. But on that quiet

July 31, 1945, no-one had even heard of such a thing as an atomic bomb. They soon would, though.

Shortly after leaving Eniwetok, *Uganda* crossed the International Dateline, and it was July 31 all over again. This "July 32" was the 140th day since *Uganda's* lines had touched a jetty. On the run to Pearl Harbor there was time to shake out kit and to clean and press blue uniforms not used since Alexandria. The great American base where the Pacific war began was reached on August 4. *Uganda* stopped long enough to fuel and take on supplies before continuing eastward. No one went ashore.

*Uganda* was between Pearl Harbor and Esquimalt when the atomic bombs which brought World War II to a quick and fiery conclusion exploded over Hiroshima and Nagasaki. At 0530 on August 10, 1945, about seventy miles off Esquimalt, HMCS *Uganda* was met by the corvette HMCS *Shediac* who turned to escort the cruiser to harbour. Four hours later *Uganda* secured to the ammunition jetty in the port that Vernon knew well from his days in *Prince David*.

No band greeted the ship; no citizens turned out to cheer the returning sailors. The ship's company had not expected a welcome and did not much care. There was a final kit search before they left the ship - a last attempt to find the Colts. They got their gear together - seabags and hammocks - mustered on deck, received their travel warrants and boarded transport to Vancouver. By 1900 they were on a train headed east, no longer a ship's company; just sailors going home on leave.

Vernon arrived back on Prince Edward Island August 17, 1945, possibly the first Drake since Sir Francis to have encircled the globe, and that in slightly less than one year. Officially, he was on leave; in reality the war was over for him. His service in the Royal Canadian Naval Volunteer Reserve ended on October 22, 1945, with an honourable discharge at HMCS *Queen Charlotte* in Charlottetown, where he had enlisted five years, one month and four days previously. He had spent four years, one month and thirteen days of his enlistment in three warships on active service on four oceans. For his service he was subsequently awarded the following medals:

> Canadian Volunteer Service Medal (CVSM);
> Victory Medal;
> 1939 -45 Star;
> Atlantic Star;
> Pacific Star.

In 1994 he received the Lower Normandy Commemorative Medal awarded to D-Day veterans by L'Association Debarquement et Bataille de Normandie 1944, Abbaye-aux-Dames, Caen.

# EPILOGUE.

On July 28, the day after *Uganda* detached, Task Force 37 bombarded installations on Honshu, the main Japanese home island. Again, on August 9, a portion of the Task Force designated TU 38.1.8 - *Newfoundland, Gambia, Terpsichore, Tenacious* and *Termigant* - attacked Kamaishi on Honshu. On this day, too, Lieut. Robert Hampton Gray D.S.C., RCNVR, flying off HMS *Formidable*, lost his life attacking and sinking a Japanese destroyer in Onagawa Wan. He was posthumously awarded the Victoria Cross, November 12, 1945.

For some time the Japanese Emperor and the more moderate elements of the Imperial Government had been convinced of the necessity of ending the war and were seeking to bring the die-hard militarists to their point of view. On August 10, following the bombing of Nagasaki, the inevitability of surrender was accepted. Capitulation came on August 14, even as the US Third Fleet kept up its attacks. On August 15 further strikes were cancelled as the entire Allied world celebrated VJ-Day.

On August 12 the bulk of the BPF detached for Sydney via Manus. *King George V, Indefatigable, Gambia, Newfoundland, Troubridge, Termigant, Tenacious, Teazer, Terpsichore, Barfleur, Napier, Nizam, Wakeful* and *Wrangler* remained to represent the Empire among the 258 warships gathered in Tokyo Bay on September 2, 1945. On the wide quarterdeck of USS *Missouri*, in a ceremony orchestrated by General Douglas MacArthur, representatives of His Imperial Majesty Emperor Hirohito of Japan and representatives of the Allied Powers signed the instrument of surrender. Admiral Sir Bruce Fraser signed for Great Britain. As Commander-in-Chief of the British Pacific Fleet, he had earned the right. Captain Rollo Mainguy RCN who, as HMCS *Uganda's* Captain, had surely earned the right to sign for Canada, was not there; Colonel L. Moore-Cosgrove, the Canadian Military Attache in Australia, signed[1] (albeit on the line for "Belgium"!). When the last pen had been laid down General MacArthur, spoke the final words: "Let us pray that peace be now restored to the world and that God will preserve it always. These proceedings are now closed."[2]

For Canada, World War II had lasted 2,187 days. More than a million Canadian men and women enlisted in the armed forces. More than 45,000 gave their lives. The navy in which Vernon served had grown to be the world's third largest; our air force was the world's fourth largest, and our army numbered six divisions. All this from a nation of eleven million.

On the grand scale of world-wide involvement, it had been the costliest war in human history. Seventy million men and women had taken up arms; seventeen million of them had died; eighteen million more civilians were killed or died from war's effects. The computable cost in treasure exceeded a trillion dollars; the unmeasurable costs were far greater. In his broadcast to the American people from the *Missouri* after the surrender ceremony MacArthur concluded with these words: "We have had our last chance. If we do not devise some greater and more equitable system [to resolve disputes between nations] Armageddon will be at our door...It must be of the spirit if we are to save the flesh."

Vernon was at home. With the rest of *Uganda's* crew, he was among the first of Canada's surviving veterans to be there. Neither he nor the ships in which he had sailed would ever again ply hostile waters. For the sailor and the ships new lives were ahead; out of the stuff of former days memories were already formed.

After the Normandy invasion, *Prince David* participated in Operation "Dragoon", the invasion of Southern France. She was mined December 10, 1944 off Aegia Island, Greece, and was repaired at Ferryville, Algeria, leaving there in March 1945 for refit at Esquimalt. She was paid off in June 1945 and laid up in Lynn Creek until she was sold to the Charlton Steam Shipping Co., who refitted her, renamed her *Charlton Monarch* and put her to work in general immigrant and freight trade between the United Kingdom, Europe, Africa and South America. She was broken up in 1951 at Swansea.

The other two Princes outlived *David*: *Prince Robert* was also sold to the Charlton company at the same time as *Prince David* and was renamed *Charlton Sovereign*. She was put on a Far East route until sold again in 1952 to Fratelli Grimaldi Sicula Oceanica and renamed *Lucania*. She was broken up at Vado in 1962. As noted earlier, *Prince Henry* was handed over to the Royal Navy in April 1945. As *Empire Parkston* she toiled as a troop ship between Harwich and the Hook of Holland. She was broken up at La Spezia in 1962.

HMS *Glasgow* saw no more war service after going to the Tyne in 1944, her refit not being completed until after VE-Day. She went to the East Indies Station in 1945, and to the Americas and West Indies Station in 1948. (Unknown to Vernon, she was in Halifax in August 1949 to take part in that city's bicentennial celebrations.) Late in 1951 she joined the Mediterranean Fleet. As Admiral Lord Mountbatten's flagship she was in the Coronation Naval Review at Spithead on June 15, 1953. Assignment to the Home Fleet followed in 1955. In November 1956 she went into Reserve at Portsmouth. On July 4, 1958, British Iron and Steel Corporation began breaking her up at Blyth, just north of Newcastle-on-Tyne.

HMS *Sheffield*, the "Shiny Sheff", returned from Boston to Portsmouth in May 1945, going into refit there for another year. She performed a variety of peace time assignments with the Home Fleet, on the America and West Indies Station and the Mediterranean. She went out of commission in 1964, was purchased by Shipbreaking Industries Ltd. in 1967 and was broken up at Faslane.

HMCS *Uganda* refitted at Esquimalt from August 10, 1945 until January 25, 1946. As a training ship for junior officers and new entry personnel, she departed Esquimalt February 5 1946 to cruise down the west coast of South America and around Cape Horn (a voyage Vernon would have appreciated). She called at the Falkland Islands and various east coast South American ports, returning to Esquimalt via the Panama Canal. On August 1 1947 she was paid off to Reserve. She was brought out of Reserve, refitted and recommissioned HMCS *Quebec* on January 14 1952. She sailed for Halifax on March 11.

She participated in various NATO exercises during 1952, and was flagship of the Canadian Coronation Squadron at Spithead in June 1953. She was part of NATO Exercise "Mariner" in September, 1953, then went into refit until March 1954. After a time in the Caribbean she left on January 4 1955 to circumnavigate Africa. In the course of this voyage she traversed the Suez Canal in the opposite direction from her first transit ten years previously.

Back in Halifax by mid-April, 1955, she had one more exercise with NATO forces before finally paying off on June 13 1956. She was purchased by a Japanese firm for breakup, beginning in February, 1961.

HMCS *Uganda's* wartime ship's company scattered far and wide. A few of her officers, such as Captain Mainguy, Commander Pullen and Lieutenant Landymore, remained in the Navy and attained Flag rank. Others, such as Lieutenant John Robarts, had distinguished careers in civilian life. The vast majority of the crew returned to the cares, demands, opportunities and anonymity of civilian life. Of the Prince Edward Islanders in *Uganda*, only Jim Grady returned to military life.

After his discharge, Vernon invested his service gratuities in a small taxi business in Charlottetown, but after three years he sold out to a partner, went to Montreal, joined the International Seafarers Union and went back to sea. In the merchant ships *Riverside, Angusdale* and *Federal Mariner* he recrossed many of the seas, and revisited many of the ports he had known as a young sailor in the Navy. In 1952 he came home from the sea to help his father on the family farm, but the partnership ended with his father's untimely death in 1957. For the next nine years Vernon worked as a serviceman at a car dealership in Charlottetown. Then an opportunity opened for him on the CN Marine ferries operating between Borden, Prince Edward Island and Cape Tormentine, New Brunswick. Starting as a deckhand, it was not long before he was on the wheel as a quartermaster. It is doubtful whether the ferry boat sailors who were his mates, experienced only in relatively calm inland waters, ever believed his stories of storms at sea. He retired from Marine Atlantic, as the ferry service had come to be known, in 1982.

The HMCS *Uganda* Veteran's Association held its first reunion July 31 to August 2 1970, at HMCS *York*, in Toronto. Biennial reunions since then, and a regular newsletter, have maintained ties between many former shipmates, but Vernon has not been one of that number, and his contacts with old friends have been sparse.

Persistent representations to Government for special recognition, by medal or certificate, of this singular group of Canadians who formed the country's only effective fighting unit against the Japanese have been ignored. Their service is acknowledged by the Pacific Star.

HMCS *Uganda* gained lasting notoriety as the only fighting ship ever to have voted herself out of action. The ship and her crew were stigmatized, but after more than half a century the stigma seems unfair. The ship's service record was excellent. Her crew never refused an order, never shirked their duty. They were praised by Admiral and Vice-Admiral. From this distance it seems that the ship and her company were pawns manipulated by the highest level politicians, against the best advice of their naval experts, to serve short term political strategies.

The decision of sixty-six percent of *Uganda's* people not to volunteer for service in the Pacific has been unfavourably compared to the eighty-five percent of *Prince Robert's* crew who volunteered, without considering that *Uganda* was there, and *Prince Robert* was going there. Moreover, Captain Creery in *Prince Robert* had a strong emotional card to play: as an AMC, his ship had escorted the ill-fated Canadian infantry force to Hong Kong late in 1941. Should they not now do what they could to hasten the survivors' return?

Many of *Uganda's* crew were long serving Volunteer Reserves; they went to the Pacific expecting to stay as long as orders required them to stay. But given a choice (who had ever thought of such an eventuality?) and weighing the merits of going home or staying in the discomfort and danger of the Pacific theatre of war, how else would many of the tired, lonesome, home-sick young men have chosen? That Vernon and a few hundred others chose to see things through to the end does not render their decision less understandable. It did, however, bring their ship's wartime service to an inglorious conclusion. The crowning irony was that, had *Uganda* stayed just a few more days in the Pacific, the swiftly rushing tide of events would have carried her and her crew to the honour they had fairly earned. The best that can be said is that this was one irony of war which cost no lives. Perhaps the whole sorry business was the curse for retaining her original name when *Uganda* became an HMC Ship.

1. Henry H. Adams, Years to Victory, 473.
2   Ibid.

*Fellow Petty Officers, including Richard Curley, bear the body of P.O. Dumont aft for Burial Service and committal June 26, 1945.*

*a). HMCS <u>Uganda's</u> crew on the quarterdeck for the service of burial at sea. On starboard side from the left: buglers; rifle party; commital party; bearers.*
*b). Honor guard facing outboard with arms reversed as the Chaplain reads the pre-commital prayer.*

# BIBLIOGRAPHY.

All of the following books were useful to me, in one way or another, in the preparation of this book, and I acknowledge here my debt to all their authors.

Adams, Henry H.. Years to Victory. New York: David MacKay Company Inc., 1973.

Ambrose, Stephen E., D-day, June 6, 1944. The Climactic Battle of World War II. New York: Simon & Shuster, 1994.

Belote, James, and Belote, William. Typhoon of Steel: The Battle for Okinawa. New York: Harper & Row, 1970.

Bennett, Geoffrey. Naval Battles of World War II. London: B.T. Batsford, 1975.

Blumenson, Martin. Liberation. World War II. Alexandria, Virginia: Time-Life Books, 1978.

Butcher, Alan D. I Remember Haida. Hantsport, N.S.: Lancelot Press, 1985.

Donaldson, Richard L. "Naval Training 1910 - 1985". Canada's Navy, a special edition of Wings Magazine. Calgary: Corvus Publishing Group, 1985.

Foster, J.A.. Heart of Oak A Pictorial History of the Royal Canadian Navy. Toronto: Methuen, 1985.

Geneja, Stephen Conrad. The Cruiser Uganda One War - Many Conflicts. Corbyville,Ontario: Tyendinaga Publishers, 1994.

German, Tony. The Sea Is At Our Gates The History of the Canadian Navy. Toronto: McClelland & Stewart, 1990.

Gray, Edwyn. Operation Pacific. The Royal Navy's War Against Japan 1941 - 1945.Annapolis, Maryland: Naval Institute Press, 1989.

Hannington, Daniel. "75 Years of Naval Training". Canada's Navy, a special edition of Wings Magazine. Calgary: Corvus Publishing Group, 1985.

Kemp, Anthony. D-Day and the Invasion of Normandy. Discoveries. Harry N. Abrams Inc., 1994.

Lamb, James B. On the Triangle Run, Don Mills, Ontario: Collins Paperbacks, 1989. Manual of Seamanship, Vol. I. Ottawa: King's Printer, 1937.

McKee, Fraser M., "Princes Three. Canada's Use of Armed Merchant Cruisers During World War II". RCN In Retrospect, Edited by James A. Boutilier. Vancouver: UBC Press, 1982.

MacPherson, Ken and Burgess, John.The Ships of Canada's Naval Forces 1910 - 1981. Toronto: Collins, 1981.

Pope, Dudley. 73 North. The Battle of the Barents Sea. London: Weidenfeld and Nicholson, 1958.

Ryan, Cornelius. The Longest Day  June 6,1944. New York: Simon & Shuster, 1959.

Salmaggi, Cesare and Pallavisini, Alfredo.  2194 Days of War. New York: Gallery Books, 1988.

Shull, Joseph.  The Far Distant Ships. Ottawa: Queen's Printer, 1952.

Stephen, Martin. The Fighting Admirals. Annapolis, Maryland: Naval Institute Press, 1991

Stewart, Adrian. Guadalcanal World War II's Fiercest Naval Campaign. London: William Kimber, 1985

Tate,Warren, Costello, John and Hyde, Gerry. D-Day. New York:

Tucker, Gilbert Norman.  The Naval Service of Canada. Vol II. Ottawa: King's Printer, 1952.

Wilmot, Chester. The  Stuggle  for  Europe. London:  Collins,  1952. Collier/MacMillan, 1970.

I drew from the following unpublished materials, and am much indebted to their authors.

*Midshipman's Personal Log, April 19/44 to July 10/44.* Commander Colin Balfour, RN

*Personal Diary, November 6/44 to August 1/45.* AB Robert Cross, RCNVR.

*Personal Diary, June 1/44 to June 26/44.* AB R.E. Hughes, RN.

*Ships I Have Sailed and Bastards I Have Known.* Selected memoirs of PO Richard Curley, RCNVR, as related by Janet Christian, March 4, 1993.

*Letter To His Parents June 14/44.* Lieut. Comm. McNab, RN.

*Personal Diary, May 19/44 to September 2/44.* AB Bill O'Neil, RCNVR.

In addition, I had delightful and informative conversations with the following RCNVR veterans:

L\Ck Frank Carragher.
OS James Grady.
AB Patrick Horgan.
AB Joseph LeClair.
AB Jack Thompson.

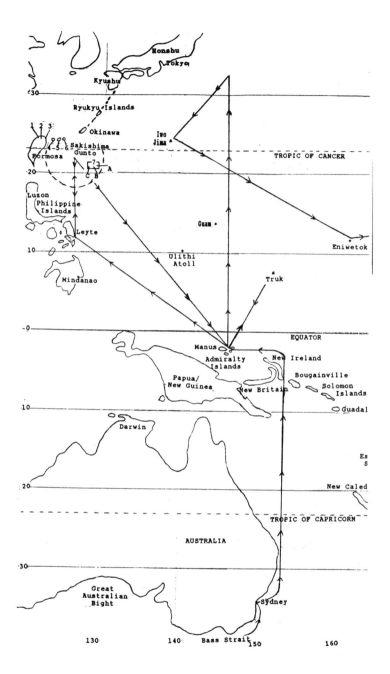

*HMCS <u>Uganda</u> in the Pacific, March 24, 1945 - July 27, 1945. Diagrammatic, the actual courses are not plotted. The dotted half-circle encloses the principal area of operations and fueling: 1. Shenchiku; 2. Hiirun; 3. Matsuyama; 4. Iriomote; 5. Ishigaki; 6. Miyako; 7. Fueling Area - A. Cootie; B. Midge; C. Mosquito.*

# APPENDIX A.

Royal Canadian Navy ships present at D-Day,
or assigned to Invasion Duties.

Source: MacPherson, Ken and John Burgess, *The Ships of Canada's Naval Forces 1910 - 1981.* Collins, Toronto, 1981.

Landing Ships (Infantry).

*Prince David*
*Prince Henry*

Destroyers.

*Algonquin*
*Chaudiere*
*Gatineau*
*Haida*
*Huron*
*Kootenay*
*Iroquois*
*Ottawa (2nd)*
*Qu'Appelle*
*Restigouche*
*Sioux*
*Skeena*
*St. Laurent*

Frigates.

*Cape Breton*
*Grou*
*Matane*
*Outremont*
*Port Colborne*
*St. John*
*Stormont*
*Swansea*
*Teme*
*Waskesiu*

Corvettes

*Alberni*
*Calgary*
*Camrose*
*Kitchener*
*Drumheller*
*Louiusburg* (2nd)
*Lunenburg*
*Mayflower*
*Mimico*

Corvettes, cont'd

*Prescott*
*Port Arthur*
*Regina*
*Rimouski*
*Summerside*
*Trentonian*
*Woodstock*

Bangor Minesweepers
*Bayfield*
*Blairmore*
*Canso*
*Caraquet*
*Fort William*
*Georgian*
*Guysborough*
*Kenora*
*Malpeque*
*Milltown*
*Minas*
*Mulgrave*
*Thunder*
*Vegreville*
*Wasaga*

29th MTB Flotilla
*459, 466, 485, 486, 491.*

65th MTB Flotilla
*726, 727, 735, 743, 797, 448*

1st Canadian Flotilla LCI (L)
*117, 121, 166, 249, 266, 277, 285, 298, 301.*

2nd Canadian Flotilla LCI (L)
*115, 118, 135, 250, 252, 262, 263, 276, 299, 306.*

3rd Canadian Flotilla LCI (L)
*125, 255, 270, 271, 288, 295, 302, 305, 310, 311.*